Frommer's®

W9-AWE-752

Venice
day BY day

1st Edition

by Stephen Brewer

Wiley Publishing, Inc.

Contents

Published by:

Wiley Publishing, Inc.

111 River St.
Hoboken, NJ 07030-5774

ISBN-13: 978-0-7645-9952-1

ISBN-10: 0-7645-9952-6

Editor: Alexis Lipsitz Flippin

Production Editor: M. Faunette Johnston

Photo Editor: Richard Fox

Cartographer: Andrew Murphy

Savvy Traveler illustrations by Rashell Smith and Karl Brandt

Production by Wiley Indianapolis Composition Services

For information on our other products and services or to obtain technical support, please contact our Customer Care Department within the U.S. at 800/762-2974, outside the U.S. at 317/572-3993 or fax 317/572-4002.

Wiley also publishes its books in a variety of electronic formats. Some content that appears in print may not be available in electronic formats.

Manufactured in China

5   4

A Note from the Publisher

Organizing your time. That's what this guide is all about.

Other guides give you long lists of things to see and do and then expect you to fit the pieces together. The Day by Day guides are different. These guides tell you the best of everything, and then they show you how to see it in the smartest, most time-efficient way. Our authors have designed detailed itineraries organized by time, neighborhood or special interest. And each tour comes with a bulleted map that takes you from stop to stop.

Hoping to relive the glory days of the Republic of Venice, or to tour the highlights of the Gallerie dell'Accademia? Planning a walk through Piazza San Marco, or a whirlwind tour of the very best that Venice has to offer? Whatever your interest or schedule, the Day by Days give you the smartest route to follow. Not only do we take you to the top sights and attractions, but we introduce you to those special moments that only locals know about—those "finds" that turn tourists into travelers.

The Day by Days are also your top choice if you're looking for one complete guide for all your travel needs. The best hotels and restaurants for every budget, the greatest shopping values, the wildest nightlife—it's all here.

Why should you trust our judgment? Because our authors personally visit each place they write about. They're an independent lot who say what they think and would never include places they wouldn't recommend to their best friends. They're also open to suggestions from readers. If you'd like to contact them, please send your comments my way at mspring@wiley.com, and I'll pass them on.

Enjoy your Day by Day guide — the most helpful travel companion you can buy. And have the trip of a lifetime.

Warm regards,

Michael Spring
Publisher
Frommer's Travel Guides

About the Author

Stephen Brewer stepped off a train in Venice many years ago, took one look at the Grand Canal, and decided he agreed with Marcel Proust in thinking "When I went to Venice, my dream became my address." He enjoys many other beautiful places, too, and often writes about them. He is the coauthor of *Frommer's Best Day Trips from London* and *The Unofficial Guide to England* and the forthcoming *Unofficial Guide to Ireland*, both published by Wiley, as well as other books and magazine articles.

Acknowledgments

I would like to thank the patient people at the Venice tourist office, who never seem to tire of handing out maps and telling me which vaporetto to take. Likewise, thanks to the many kindly Venetians who treat us visitors well and are always able and willing to give directions and advice. Thanks, especially, to the Venetian friends who have provided lodging over the years and introduced me to the wonders of their city, and to my talented and pleasant editor at Frommer's, Alexis Lipsitz Flippin, who's guided me through a dream of an assignment.

An Additional Note

Please be advised that travel information is subject to change at any time—and this is especially true of prices. We therefore suggest that you write or call ahead for confirmation when making your travel plans. The authors, editors, and publisher cannot be held responsible for the experiences of readers while traveling. Your safety is important to us, however, so we encourage you to stay alert and be aware of your surroundings.

Star Ratings, Icons & Abbreviations

Every hotel, restaurant, and attraction listing in this guide has been ranked for quality, value, service, amenities, and special features using a **star-rating system.** Hotels, restaurants, attractions, shopping, and nightlife are rated on a scale of zero stars (recommended) to three stars (exceptional). In addition to the star-rating system, we also use a **kids icon** to point out the best bets for families. Within each tour, we recommend cafes, bars, or restaurants where you can take a break. Each of these stops appears in a shaded box marked with a coffee cup–shaped bullet 　.

The following **abbreviations** are used for credit cards:

AE American Express	DISC Discover	V Visa
DC Diners Club	MC MasterCard	

Frommers.com

Now that you have the guidebook to a great trip, visit our website at **www. frommers.com** for travel information on more than 3,000 destinations. With features updated regularly, we give you instant access to the most current trip-planning information available. At Frommers.com, you'll also find the best prices on airfares, accommodations, and car rentals—and you can even book travel online through our travel booking partners.

A Note on Prices

Frommer's provides exact prices in each destination's local currency. As this book went to press, the rate of exchange was 1€ = US$1.30. Rates of exchange are constantly in flux; for up-to-the-minute information, consult a currency-conversion website such as www.oanda.com/convert/classic.

In the Take a Break and Best Bets section of this book, we have used a system of dollar signs to show a range of costs for one night in a hotel (the price of a double-occupancy room) or the cost of an entrée at a restaurant. Use the following table to decipher the dollar signs:

Cost	Hotels	Restaurants
$	under $100	under $10
$$	$100–$200	$10–$20
$$$	$200–$300	$20–$30
$$$$	$300–$400	$30–$40
$$$$$	over $400	over $40

An Invitation to the Reader

In researching this book, we discovered many wonderful places—hotels, restaurants, shops, and more. We're sure you'll find others. Please tell us about them, so we can share the information with your fellow travelers in upcoming editions. If you were disappointed with a recommendation, we'd love to know that, too. Please write to:

Frommer's Venice Day by Day, 1st Edition
Wiley Publishing, Inc. • 111 River St. • Hoboken, NJ 07030-5774

10 Favorite
Moments

10 Favorite **Moments**

1 Grand Canal
2 Piazza San Marco
3 Basilica of San Marco
4 Campo Santi Giovanni e Paolo
5 Rialto markets
6 The Accademia
7 Dogana da Mar customs house
8 Crossing the lagoon to Torcello
9 The Zattere
10 Ponte di Rialto

Venice, city of visual delights, fires up the imagination. The colors, the many exotic domes and mosaics, the omnipresence of water, the rich history that's almost palpable in the streets and squares—best simply to let yourself be overwhelmed by it all.

❶ Cruising on the Grand Canal. Even though the craft is a humble vaporetto (one of the city's boat buses) and the trip is an everyday routine for many Venetians, the experience never fails to be exhilarating. No matter how many times I've taken to the waters here, I'm still in awe of the dreamy water world that is Venice. *See p. 19.*

❷ Savoring Piazza San Marco. This civilized square is, as Napoleon called it, the "drawing room" of Europe. The Piazza, as it's simply known, is where Venetians and their visitors converge to sip a cappuccino or cocktail on the outdoor terraces of some of Europe's grandest cafes. *See p. 41, bullet* ❶.

❸ Being dazzled by the mosaics in San Marco. Step into the basilica and let the shimmering brilliance of thousands of mosaics sweep you away. Then take a close look at the glass tiles that cover the floors, walls, and domes. The saints and sinners, angels, and mere mortals so painstakingly

The sinuous sweep of Venice's Grand Canal.

depicted here are touchingly human. *See p 23, bullet* ❶.

❹ Sipping a cappuccino in Campo Santi Giovanni e Paolo. Grab an outdoor table at Rosa Salva, a venerable cafe, and soak in the scene. Verrocchio's equestrian statue of Bartolomeo Colleoni stands guard over the neighborhood, and the formidable facade of the Chiesa di Santi Giovanni e Paolo hints at the treasures that await you. *See p 41, bullet* ❹.

❺ Strolling through the Rialto markets. Exotic sea creatures from the Adriatic, artichokes from the island of Sant' Erasmo in the lagoon, and freshly picked pears from the Veneto seem especially appetizing with the Grand Canal flowing past. The sheer bustle of this place, the commercial heart of Venice for more than 1,000 years, brings to mind old Shylock's oft-quoted question in *The Merchant of Venice*, "What's news on the Rialto?" *See p 42, bullet* ❺.

Fresh radicchio for sale in the Rialto vegetable market.

6 **Standing in front of your favorite painting in the Accademia (or in any other museum of scuola, for that matter).** You'll soon find the canvas that captivates you. Some worthy candidates are Giorgione's mysterious *La Temptesta* or Carpaccio's rich *Story of Saint Ursula and Miracles of the Relic of the True Cross*. If you're anything like me, you'll find yourself mesmerized by more than one. *See p 31.*

7 **Looking over the Grand Canal and Bacino di San Marco from the Dogana da Mar, the Customs house.** On this point of land where ships once moored to be inspected, with the sea lanes stretching in front of you, it's easy to imagine Venice as a seafaring power and the crossroads between East and West. Magnificent relics of the trading wealth that once poured into the city complete the view. *See p 19, bullet* **1**.

8 **Crossing the lagoon to Torcello.** Part of the charm of Torcello is the ghostlike presence of the 20,000 souls who once inhabited this all-but-deserted little island; they left behind the glorious, mosaic-paved Basilica di Santa Maria

The Ponte di Rialto at night.

The Basilica di Santa Maria Assunta, on the island of Torcello.

Assunta, one of few remaining signs of civilization. Past grandeur aside, Torcello is also a perfectly nice place to escape from the bustle of Venice for an afternoon. *See p 45, bullet* **7**.

9 **Taking a passeggiata on the Zattere.** Many Venetians couldn't imagine ending a day without an evening stroll on this broad promenade along the Giudecca Canal, and you should join them. Ochre-colored houses capture the last rays of the sun, a tangy sea breeze stirs the air, and the church of Il Redentore across the canal provides a stage-set backdrop. *See p 86, bullet* **2**.

10 **Standing on the Ponte di Rialto at night.** Who cares if the gondolas slipping beneath your feet are laden with sightseers and the strains of "O Solo Mio" are taped? Fall under the spell of the shimmering reflections on the *palazzi* and imagine a time when the likes of Lord Byron and Casanova glided up the canal in the dark of a Venetian night. *See p. 48, bullet* **2**. ●

The Best of Venice in One Day

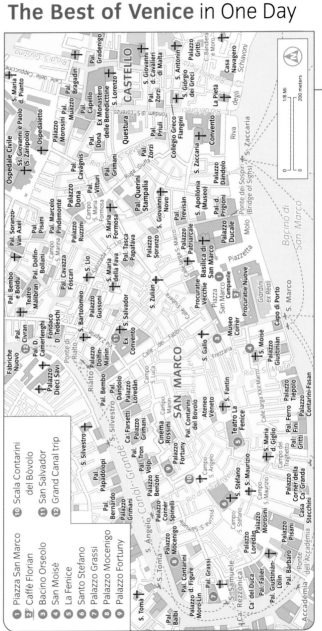

1 Piazza San Marco
2P Caffè Florian
3 Bacino Orseolo
4 San Moisè
5 La Fenice
6 Santo Stefano
7 Palazzo Grassi
8 Palazzo Mocenigo
9 Palazzo Fortuny
10 Scala Contarini del Bóvolo
11 San Salvador
12 Grand Canal trip

The French novelist **Marcel Proust** said of his first trip to Venice, "My dream became my address." You may feel the same way as you walk into the Piazza San Marco and begin to explore the city. Not far from the piazza are uniquely Venetian palaces and churches. Top off your tour with a cruise along one of the world's most storied waterways, the Grand Canal. START: **Piazza San Marco.**

① ★★★ **Piazza San Marco.** The heart of the city for more than 1,000 years combines the very old (the basilica) with the relatively new (the 16th- and 17th-c. Procuratie Vecchie and Procuratie Nuove on the north and south sides of the square), yet still manages to be harmonious.

② **Caffè Florian.** You'll pay dearly for your cappuccino on the terrace, but you'll never sip coffee in more atmospheric surroundings. *Piazza San Marco.* ☎ 041-5205641. See p 113.

A child feeds the pigeons in Piazza San Marco.

③ ★★ **Bacino Orseolo.** One of the city's eight gondola stations is a good place to get a close look at these uniquely Venetian craft—or to board one. ⏱ *15 min. Fondamenta Orseolo. San Marco/ Vallaresso.*

④ ★ **San Moisè.** In a city of beautiful churches, this baroque extravagance stands out as one of the ugliest. ⏱ *30 min. Campo San Moisè.* ☎ 041-5285840. Daily 3:30– 7pm. San Marco/Vallaresso.

⑤ ★★ **La Fenice.** The aptly named opera house (Fenice means Phoenix) has burned several times, most recently in 1996, and risen from the ashes looking just as it has for centuries. Several Verdi operas, including *Rigoletto* and *La Traviata*, premiered in the sumptuous, newly restored house, and Maria Callas is among the stars who have graced the stage. ⏱ *15 min. Campo San Fantin. www. teatrolafenice.it. See p 122 for tour and ticket information. Vaporetto: Santa Maria del Giglio.*

Inside Venice's glorious opera house, La Fenice.

Piazza San Marco

In the **1A Museo Correr,** maps, coins, costumes, and, best of all, paintings by Vittore Carpaccio (room 38) and Jacopo Bellini (room 36) recall the days of the Republic. *See p 31, bullet 1.* Bronze moors strike the hour on the **1B Torre dell'Orologio;** during Ascension and Epiphany the Magi make an hourly appearance at this clock tower accompanied by a procession of angels. In the **1C Piazzetta dei Leoncini,** marble lions stand guard over what was once a marketplace. The Byzantine **1D Basilica di San Marco** inspired 19th-century man of letters John Ruskin to exhale into his journals, "The crests of the arches break into a marble foam, and toss themselves into the blue sky in flashes and wreaths of sculpted spray"; less poetical observers will be similarly moved. *See p 23, bullet 1.* **1E Palazzo Ducale,** the palace where the doges lived and ruled, is majestic but has a touch of whimsy as well. *See p 37, bullet 1.* The city's tallest structure, the **1F Campanile,** affords stunning views. *See p 44, bullet 2.* Two columns, one topped by a winged lion and the other by St. Theodore, frame the **1G Piazzetta San Marco,** the seaside extension of Piazza San Marco. One of Venice's great Renaissance monuments, the **1H Biblioteca Marciana** was completed in the 16th century to house a precious hoard of Greek and Latin manuscripts. ⏲ *4–5 hr.*

6 ★ Santo Stefano. Beyond a 15th-century sculpted portal by Bartolomeo Bon is a wooden ceiling whose shape resembles the inverted hull of a ship and two works by Tintoretto in the sacristy. ⏱ *30 min. Campo Santo Stefano.* ☎ *041-5225061. Sacristy 2€. Church daily 9am–7pm; sacristy Mon–Sat 10am–5pm, Sun 1–5pm. Vaporetto: San Samuele.*

7 ★★ Palazzo Grassi. One of the last of the great palaces to be built in Venice dates from 1749 and was stunningly converted in the 1980s into the city's venue for traveling art shows and other special exhibitions. *San Marco 3231, San Samuele.* ☎ *041-5231680. www.palazzograssi.it. Prices and times vary by exhibition. Vaporetto: San Samuele.*

8 ★ Palazzo Mocenigo. One of the largest and grandest houses in Venice is actually four palaces that a succession of prominent residents combined over the centuries. Lord Byron lived here in 1818–19 with enough pets to populate a small zoo, an army of servants, and his mistress. He often swam home across the lagoon from outings on the Lido. ⏱ *10 min. Not open to the public. Calle Mocenigo. Vaporetto: San Stae.*

9 ★ Palazzo Fortuny. The last resident was textile designer and photographer Mariano Fortuny. The 15th-century palazzo now displays his distinctive work. ⏱ *1 hr. Campo San Beneto. See p 37, bullet* **3**. *Vaporetto: San Angelo.*

10 ★★ Scala Contarini del Bòvolo. A beautiful spiral staircase (*bòvolo*, or snail, in Venetian dialect) climbs five stories from a lovely

Fanciful loggia of the Palazzo Ducale.

courtyard. At the top is a panoramic view over the rooftops of Venice. ⏱ *30 min. Corte di Contarini del Bòvolo.* ☎ *041-5217521. Apr–Oct daily 10am–6pm; Nov–Mar Sat–Sun 10am–4pm. Vaporetto: Rialto.*

11 ★ San Salvador. The handsome white interior provides refuge from the busy Mercerie, one of Venice's main shopping streets, as well as the chance to view some excellent paintings: Two Titians, a *Transfiguration* and an *Annunciation,* and Carpaccio's *Disciples at Emmaus.* ⏱ *30 min. Campo San Salvador.* ☎ *041-2702464. Mon–Sat 9am–noon, 3–6pm; Sun 4–6pm. Vaporetto: Rialto.*

12 ★★★ Grand Canal trip. A cruise up one of the world's most beautiful waterways is the ideal way to end a long day of touring. Get off at the Ferrovia stop for the return trip. ⏱ *1½ hr. See p 18 for what to look for on the Grand Canal; see p 161 for details on the vaporetto. Vaporetto: San Marco/Vallaresso.*

The Best of Venice in Two Days

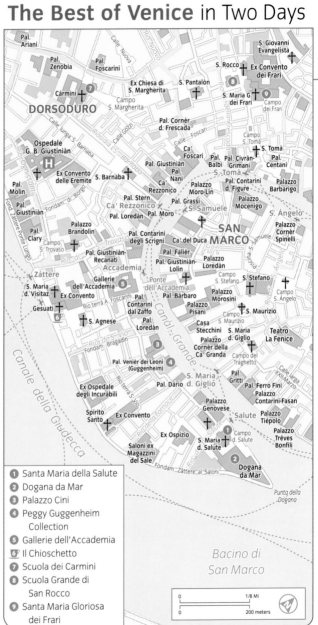

1 Santa Maria della Salute
2 Dogana da Mar
3 Palazzo Cini
4 Peggy Guggenheim Collection
5 Gallerie dell'Accademia
6 Il Chioschetto
7 Scuola dei Carmini
8 Scuola Grande di San Rocco
9 Santa Maria Gloriosa dei Frari

Now it's time to **explore the quarters** across the Grand Canal from San Marco. This is not a quiet neighborhood amble: Some of Venice's greatest masterpieces are here, and you'll discover one remarkable church and treasure-filled museum after another.
START: **Salute**

1 ★★ Santa Maria della Salute. Saint Mary of Health was begun in 1630, an offering of thanks to the Virgin Mary for bringing an end to a plague outbreak that killed a third of the city's population. The massive white-marble church by architect Baldassare Longhena commands the entrance to the Grand Canal, and its high domes mimic those of San Marco across the water and suggest the Madonna's crown. A suitably impressive collection of paintings hang in the round, marble interior, including Tintoretto's *Wedding at Cana* and Titian's *St. Mark Enthroned with Saints.* The Virgin is honored on the high altar with a Byzantine icon and a wonderfully dramatic marble sculptural group by Giusto Le Corte—an old hag representing the plague flees from a torch-bearing angel as the Virgin and a noblewoman, in the role of Venice, look on. ⏱ *30 min. Campo della Salute.* ☎ *041-5225558. Sacristy: 1.50€. Apr–Sept daily 9am–noon, 3–6:30pm; Oct–Mar daily 9am–noon, 3–5:30pm. Vaporetto: Salute.*

2 ★★ La Dogana da Mar. The 17th-century Customs house at the tip of the Dorsoduro resembles the hull of a ship and was once a mandatory stop for all ships entering Venice. On the roof, a statue of Fortune stands over a gold globe, and looking out to sea from the landing stage it's easy to imagine the time when Venetians felt they were indeed the lucky rulers of the waves. ⏱ *30 min. Vaporetto: Salute.*

3 ★★ Palazzo Cini. Industrialist Vittorio Cini (1885–1977) spent

The church of Santa Maria della Salute.

much of his fortune collecting religious art from Tuscany, and his small, intimate palace is filled with works by Sandro Botticelli, Piero della Francesca, and others. ⏱ 45 min. *Campo Carità.* ☎ *041-5222247. See p 37, bullet* **4**. *Vaporetto: Accademia.*

4 ★★★ Peggy Guggenheim Collection. The American heiress spent much of her life collecting contemporary art, living up to her pledge to "buy a picture a day." In 1949 she found a home for herself and her paintings, the Palazzo Venier dei Leoni, that is as surreal as some of the paintings she preferred. Only the ground floor of the 18th-century palace was completed, providing distinctive surroundings for a collection that includes Giorgio De Chirico's *The Red Tower,* Rene Magritte's *Empire of Light,* and

Heavenly Bodies, *a painting by Rufino Tamayo, in the Peggy Guggenheim Collection.*

works by Jackson Pollock (whom Guggenheim discovered), Max Ernst (whom she married), and many others. The shady garden is filled with sculpture as well as the graves of Guggenheim and her dogs. The

Giovanni Bellini's Madonna of the Red Cherubs, *in the Gallerie dell'Accademia.*

waterside terrace provides sweeping views up and down the Grand Canal. 🕐 *1 hr. Palazzo Venier dei Leoni.* ☎ *041-2405411. www. guggenheim-venice.it.10€. Wed–Mon 10am–6pm. Vaporetto: Accademia.*

⑤ ★★★ Gallerie dell'Accademia. A walk through the galleries can take a good part of a day and is a lesson in Venetian art, from Carpaccio to Tiepolo. If time is tight or the temptation to be outdoors exploring the city too great, at least see Room 10, where works by Titian, Tintoretto, and Veronese line the walls, and Room 21, for a look at Carpaccio's colorful action-filled *Story of Saint Ursula* cycle. 🕐 *2–3 hr. Campo Carità. See p 34 for full details. Vaporetto: Accademia.*

⑥ Il Chioschetto. A panino and a glass of wine, well deserved after a morning of viewing art, come with a view of the Giudecca Canal. *Zattere Ponte Luongo.* ☎ *338-1174077.*

Back to Scuola

Founded in the Middle Ages, the Venetian *scuole* (schools) were guilds that brought together merchants and craftspeople in certain trades (Scuola dei Carmini: dyers), as well as those who shared similar religious devotions (Scuola Grande di San Rocco). The guilds were social clubs, credit unions, and sources of spiritual guidance. Many commissioned elaborate headquarters and hired the best artists of the day to decorate them. The *scuole* that remain in Venice today house some of the city's finest art treasures.

7 ★★ **Scuola dei Carmini.** The Carmelite order founded this *scuola* in the 17th century in association with the guild of dyers and hired the architect Baldassare Longhena to build their premises. The master's facades remain intact—as does much of the interior, little touched over the centuries. A painting by Tiepolo, *The Virgin in Glory Appearing to the Blessed Simon Stock,* flows over the ceiling of the salon. ⏱ *30 min. Campo dei Carmini. See p 32, bullet* **8**. *Vaporetto: San Basilio.*

8 ★★★ **Scuola Grande di San Rocco.** San Rocco, the patron saint of the sick and a Venetian favorite, was especially popular for his alleged prowess at curing the plague. The *scuola* was begun in the early 16th century to house the saint's relics. ⏱ *30 min. Campo San Rocco. See p 32, bullet* **9**. *Vaporetto: San Tomà.*

9 ★★★ **Santa Maria Gloriosa dei Frari** One of the largest churches in Venice is also one of the city's great treasure troves of art, with masterworks by Titian and Giovanni Bellini. ⏱ *1 hr. Campo dei Frari. See p 33, bullet* **10**. *Vaporetto: San Tomà.*

The church of Santa Maria Gloriosa dei Frari.

The Best of Venice in Three Days

1. Rialto
2a. Alla Madonna
3. Traghetto
4. Campo Santi Giovanni e Paolo (San Zanipolo)
5. Santi Apostoli
6. Strada Nuova
7. Ca d'Oro/
   Galleria Franchetti
8. Campo di Ghetto Nuovo
9. Palazzo Labia

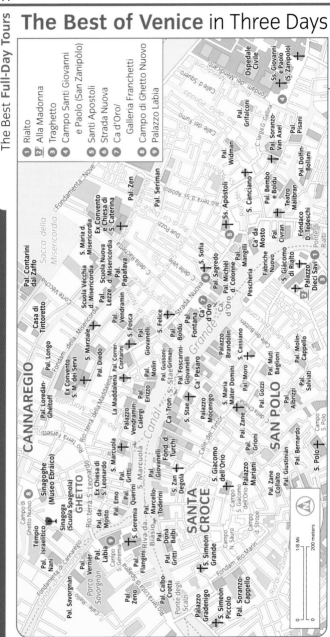

Now it's time to see everyday Venice, beginning at its busy marketplace and moving on to explore neighborhoods where Venetians go about their daily business. Along the route, too, are more of the notable churches, palaces, galleries, and monuments with which the city is so liberally laced. START: **Rialto**

1 ★★ **Rialto.** Begin the walk in the markets and alleys of the Rialto. The name comes from *rivoaltus,* or "high bank," a geographic asset when settlers in the early ninth century were searching for dry ground to establish the city's first market. The Rialto has been a commercial center ever since, the place where things happen. Ships from around the globe once docked at the Fondaco dei Tedeschi—the Renaissance-style structure that now houses the main post office—and other neighborhood warehouses, and it was here that the Grand Canal was first spanned: The Ponte dei Rialto is still the most used and appealing bridge across the canal. ⏱ *30 min. See p 43, bullet* **5A**, *for details on the Rialto markets; see p 48, bullet* **2**, *for details on the Ponte di Rialto. Vaporetto: Rialto.*

2 **Alla Madonna.** For an authentic taste of the Rialto markets, take a seat in this busy room and enjoy a seafood lunch. *Calle della Madonna.* ☎ *041-5223824. See p 98.*

3 ★ **Traghetto.** Enjoy the walk over the Ponte dei Rialto, then retrace your steps and make the crossing in one of the *traghetti* that run between the banks of the canal. A *traghetto*—basically, a large, plain gondola—provides a poor man's gondola ride (one-way passage is just .50€), but comes with a challenge—by tradition, passengers remain standing during the ride. ⏱ *10 min. Near the Rialto, traghetti run from Fondamente del Vin to Riva del Carbòn (Mon–Sat 8am–2pm) and the Pescaria to Santa Sofia (Mon–Sat 7:30am–8:30pm; Sun 8am–7pm).*

4 ★★ **Campo Santi Giovanni e Paolo (San Zanipòlo).** Bartolomeo Colleoni, a 15th-century mercenary, rides across one of Venice's most beautiful squares astride an equestrian monument by Verrocchio. The namesake basilica is the final resting place of 25 doges, entombed in marble splendor. ⏱ *45 min. Vaporetto: Fondamenta Nuove.*

A traghetto traverses the waters of the Grand Canal.

5 ★ **Santi Apostoli.** Venetian legend has it that the 12 apostles appeared to Saint Magnus and told him to build a church where he saw 12 cranes. The church's bell tower, a 17th-century addition, is topped with an onion dome and is a much-beloved landmark. Giambattista Tiepolo's rendering of Saint Lucy near the altar is eye-catching indeed—the martyr's eyes lie on the floor next to her, but she seems to be smiling all the same. ⏲ *30 min. Campo Santi Apostoli.* ☎ *041-5238297. Mon–Sat 7:30–11:30am, 5–7pm. Vaporetto: Ca' d'Oro.*

6 ★ **Strada Nuova.** One of the few straight paths in Venice (Via Garibaldi, see p 59, bullet **14**, is another) is a modern invention, laid out in the 1860s to facilitate foot traffic to and from the then-new railway station.

7 ★★★ **Ca' d'Oro/Galleria Franchetti.** A 15th-century palazzo just off the Strada Nuova still bears the trappings of a cushy Renaissance lifestyle and is filled with works by Venetian masters. ⏲ *1 hr. Calle Ca' d'Oro. See p 39, bullet **8**. Vaporetto: Ca' d'Oro.*

Tiepolo's 18th-century fresco, The Meeting of Antony and Cleopatra, *in the Palazzo Labia.*

The church of Santi Giovanni e Paolo.

8 ★★ **Campo di Ghetto Nuovo.** The Ghetto was once the only part of Venice where Jews were allowed to live. This large square and surrounding neighborhood occupy an island that was closed off at dusk and still feels remote. The houses on the square are higher than most in Venice, having been built with additional stories to accommodate a population that expanded steadily as the Jewish community prospered in trade and banking. ⏲ *15 min. Vaporetto: Ponte de Guglie.*

9 ★★ **Palazzo Labia.** One of the grandest palaces in Venice is set back from the Grand Canal—a sign that the Labias, a clan of Spanish traders, were never accepted by Venetian nobility. Giambattista Tiepolo painted a magnificent fresco of *Anthony and Cleopatra* for the Banqueting Hall in honor of the marriage of Maria Labia. ⏲ *30 min. Fondamenta Labia.* ☎ *041-5242812. Wed–Fri 3–4pm, by appointment only (call or ask your hotel to make arrangements).* ●

The Best Special-Interest Tours

Venice's **Grand Canal**

M ain Street for Venetians is this S-shaped, 2-mile-long stretch of busy waterway between San Marco and the train station. Commerce has long thrived on the canal, and for centuries nobility built their palaces on the banks. The half-hour vaporetto trip up the canal not only reveals the city's past grandeur, but also provides an exhilarating look at life in present-day Venice. START: **Vaporetto 1 from San Marco/Vallaresso toward Piazzale Roma**

1 ★ **Dogana da Mar**. The Customs house at the entrance to the Grand Canal was at one time a mandatory stop for all vessels entering Venice. *Vaporetto: Salute.*

2 ★★ **Salute.** A baroque fantasy in white marble, this church designed by Baldassare Longhena and built as an offering to end an outbreak of the plague hints at the architectural wonders that line the canal ahead. *See p 11, bullet* **1**.

3 ★ **Ca' Dario.** A long roster of former residents died under mysterious circumstances, endowing this small, 15th-century palazzo with a reputation of being cursed. *Vaporetto: Salute.*

4 ★★★ **Palazzo Venier dei Leoni/Peggy Guggenheim Collection.** The Venier clan ran into fiscal straits while building their palazzo, but the ground floor—the only part completed—was well suited to the tastes of American heiress Peggy Guggenheim. Today the palazzo shows off her collection

Venice's bustling Grand Canal.

of modern art to ideal advantage. *See p 11, bullet* **4**.

5 ★ **Palazzo Corner della Ca' Grande.** Venice's police department is headquartered in this elegant, early Renaissance palazzo built in the 1590s. *Vaporetto: Santa Maria del Giglio.*

The Dogana da Mar and the church of Santa Maria Salute.

A gondola cruises by the Ponte di Rialto.

⑥ ★ Ponte dell'Accademia. The prosaic wooden structure dates from 1934, replacing an iron structure erected in 1854—until then, the Ponte di Rialto was the only span across the canal. *Vaporetto: Accademia.*

⑦ ★★★ Gallerie dell'Accademia. Three former religious buildings house the world's richest repository of Venetian art. *See p 34.*

⑧ ★ Palazzo Grassi. The last palazzo to be built on the Grand Canal dates from 1749. Entry to one of the many exhibitions staged in the salons provides a glimpse of the beautiful courtyard and frescoed staircase. *See p 9, bullet* **⑦**.

⑨ ★ Ca' Rezzonico. The home of the Museo del Settecento Veneziano (Museum of 18th Century Venice) has also been home to the poets Robert Browning and Elizabeth Barrett Browning, Cole Porter, and James McNeill Whistler. *See p 39, bullet* **⑤**.

⑩ ★ Ca' Foscari. The home of a 15th-century doge houses the University of Venice. *Vaporetto: Ca' Rezzonico.*

⑪ ★ Palazzo Balbi. Napoleon is among the legions of spectators who have sat on the balcony to watch the many regattas that, since 1315, have crossed the finish line in front of the palazzo. *Vaporetto: San Tomà.*

⑫ ★ Palazzo Mocenigo. A clan that produced seven doges connected four adjacent palaces to create one of the grandest homes on the canal; in the early 19th century, one commodious wing accommodated Lord Byron and his menagerie. *Vaporetto: San Stae.*

⑬ ★ Palazzo Loredan and Palazzo Farsetti. Two of the first palazzi on the canal, built in the 13th century, now serve as Venice's city hall. Palazzo Loredan was home to the first woman to ever earn a college degree—she completed her studies at the University of Padua in 1678. *Vaporetto: Rialto.*

⑭ ★★★ Ponte di Rialto. Venice's most famous bridge, completed in 1590, is the first, most elegant, and busiest of the crossings over the Grand Canal. *See p 48, bullet* **②**.

⑮ ★ Fondaco dei Tedeschi. Built in 1508 as a multipurpose warehouse, office space, and a hostelry for Germans (Tedeschi) working in Venice, this Renaissance-style structure is now Venice's main post office. *Vaporetto: Rialto.*

⑯ ★ Palazzo dei Camerlenghi. The world's first-known office building was completed in 1528 for Venice's financial magistrates—a function it still serves as the headquarters of the financial court. *Vaporetto: Rialto.*

17 ★ **Fabbriche Vecchie and Fabbriche Nuove.** Both structures were built in the 15th century as warehouses. *Vaporetto: Rialto.*

18 ★ **Ca' da Mosto.** The oldest palace on the Grand Canal was completed in the 13th century for a family whose members included Alvise da Mosto, the 15th-century navigator who discovered the Cape Verde Islands. *Vaporetto: Ca d'Oro.*

19 ★ **Pescaria.** Venetians have bought their fish from this spot since the 14th century; the neo-Gothic market hall dates from the early 20th century. *See p 43. Vaporetto: Rialto.*

20 ★★ **Ca' d'Oro.** Even without the gold leaf that graced the facade and lent the palazzo its name, this early-15th-century palazzo would be a glittering example of Venetian Gothic architecture. Inside are the Venetian masterpieces of the **Galleria Franchetti**. *See p 39, bullet* **8**.

21 ★ **Ca' Pesaro.** The Pesaro family combined three Gothic houses to create one of Venice's largest palaces, now housing Asian and modern art collections. *See p 39, bullet* **6**.

22 ★ **Palazzo Vendramin Calergi.** Past residents include the composer Richard Wagner, who

The 15th-century palazzo Ca' d'Oro.

completed *Tristan and Isolde* here in 1859. The Renaissance palazzo is the winter home of the casino. *Vaporetto: Santa Marcuola.*

23 ★★ **Palazzo Labia.** The 17th-century home of a Spanish trading family now houses the Venice offices of RAI, the Italian national television network. The Labia clan left behind tales of legendary wealth and pretension—at their lavish galas, they would hurl gold dinnerware into the canal (nets laid on the canal bottom ensured easy retrieval). Another legacy: the frescoes that Giambattista Tiepolo executed for the Banqueting Hall in honor of the marriage of Maria Labia in the 18th century. *See p 16, bullet* **9**.

Mooring poles on the Grand Canal.

Best Places to See **the Byzantine**

1. Basilica di San Marco
2. Caffè Florian
3. Cloisters of Sant'Apollonia
4. Museo dell'Istituto Ellenico
5. San Giacomo di Rialto
6. San Zan Degolà
7. San Giacomo dell'Orio
8. Santa Maria e San Donato
9. Basilica di Santa Maria Assunta, Torcello
10. Santa Fosca, Torcello

ast and West come together in Venice, adding a hefty dose of exoticism to the city's cultural stew. Settlers and early traders brought with them the arts of Byzantium: church plans following the form of a Greek cross, rich mosaics, arches, and domes. The trail of the Venetian Byzantine leads from San Marco across the lagoon to the 7th-century settlement on the island of Torcello. START: **Piazza San Marco**

1 ★★★ Basilica di San Marco. Venice's Byzantine extravaganza is a shrine to the city's patron saint. Sometime around 800, or so the story goes, Venetian traders stole Mark's body from Alexandria, where he had been bishop, wrapped the remains in pork to deter Muslim guards from prying, and smuggled the prize back home. The saint soon became a symbol of the city's power. The multidomed, mosaic-paved basilica begun in the 11th century as the saint's resting place still evokes the might of the Venetian republic. See p 24.

2 Caffè Florian. Still can't get enough of the glorious mosaic facade of San Marco? Here on the terrace of one of the world's most famous cafes, you can bask in the view while lingering over a coffee. *Piazza San Marco.* ☎ 041-5205641.

3 ★ Cloisters of Sant'Apollonia. Venice's only Romanesque cloisters date from the 14th century and were once part of a Benedictine convent. Inside are Byzantine carvings and other holdings of the **Museo Diocesano di Arte Sacra.** ⏱ 30 min. Ponte della Canonica. ☎ 041-5229166. Mon–Sat 10:30am–12:30pm. Vaporetto: San Zaccaria.

4 ★ Museo dell'Istituto Ellenico. Founded by Greeks who poured into Venice after the Turks took Constantinople in 1453, the incense-scented Scuola di San Nicolo houses a hoard of icons. Many are pure Byzantine works; others show the influence of Westernized styles of painting. Next door, the campanile of the church of San Giorgio dei Greci gently leans toward a canal, supplying a vista that is uniquely Venetian. ⏱ 1 hr. Ponte dei Greci. ☎ 041-5226581. www.istitutoellenico.org. Mon–Sat 9am–12:30pm, 1–4:30pm; Sun 10am–5pm. Vaporetto: San Zaccaria.

5 ★ San Giacomo di Rialto. The oldest church in Venice, founded in the 5th century and restored in the 11th century, retains the shape of a Greek cross and other telltale Byzantine elements. A lively fruit and vegetable market is just outside the door. ⏱ 1 hr. Campo San Giacomo. ☎ 041-5224745. Mon–Sat 9:30am–noon, 4–6pm. Vaporetto: Rialto.

The spectacular interior of the Basilica di San Marco.

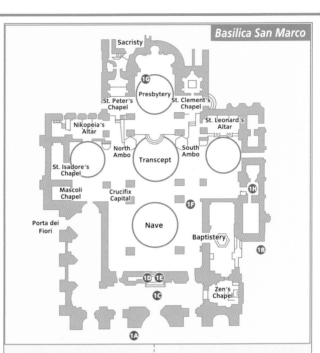

Basilica San Marco

Sacristy

St. Peter's Chapel | **1G** Presbytery | St. Clement's Chapel

St. Leonard's Altar

Nikopeia's Altar

St. Isadore's Chapel | North Ambo | Transcept | South Ambo

1H

Mascoli Chapel | Crucifix Capital | **1F**

Porta dei Fiori

Nave

Baptistery | **1B**

1D 1E

1C

Zen's Chapel

1A

In the **1A main facade** of the Basilica di San Marco, the combined effect of glittering mosaics, domes, and double rows of arches is best appreciated from the center of the piazza. Some claim that the **1B Tetrarchs,** four figures depicting Byzantine emperors, are actually infidels turned to stone while pilfering church treasures. In the **1C Atrium,** Illiterate believers boned up on the Old Testament with these lively mosaic depictions of the story of the Creation, Noah and the flood, and other biblical narratives. In the **1D Galleria,** make the climb for a close-up look at the atrium's ceiling mosaics; for the bird's-eye view of the piazza from the loggia; and to see the gilded bronze horses, loot from the Fourth Crusade, in the **1E Museo Marciano** (the horses on the loggia are copies). More than 3.8 sq. km (1½

square miles) of colorful glass-tile **1F mosaics** sparkle and bedazzle with rich renditions of an ascending Christ, saints, the apostles, and other religious rank and file. Byzantine goldsmiths fashioned the **1G Pala d'Oro,** St. Mark's final resting place, in the 10th century. Among the glittering prizes brought back from the Crusades now on view in the **1H Tesoro (Treasury)** are icons, censers (incense containers), and a relic of the true cross. ⏲ *2–3 hr. Piazza San Marco.* ☎ *041-5225205. Basilica: 1.55€; daily 9:45am–5pm (until 4:30pm Oct–Mar). Museo Marciano: 3€; daily 9:45am–5pm (until 4:30pm Oct–Mar). Pala d'Oro: 1.50€; Mon–Sat 9:45am–5pm (until 4:45pm Oct–Mar), Sun 2–5pm (1–4:45pm Oct–Mar). Tesoro: 2€; Mon–Sat 9:45am–5pm (until 4:45pm Oct–Mar), Sun 2–5pm (1–4:45pm Oct–Mar).*

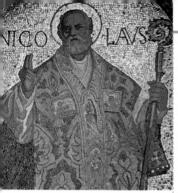

Mosaic of St. Nicholas in the Basilica di San Marco.

6 ★★ **San Zan Degolà.** One of Venice's oldest churches, built in 1007 to honor St. John the Beheaded, yielded a treasure during recent renovations: Byzantine ceiling and wall frescoes of saints and evangelists from the 11th–14th centuries. ⏱ *30 min. Campo San Zan Degolà.* ☎ *041-5240672. Mon–Sat 8am–noon. Vaporetto: Riva di Biasio.*

7 ★ **San Giacomo dell'Orio.** A 1225 renovation of this 10th-century church imparted such Byzantine/Romanesque flourishes as a charming campanile rising above the sleepy square shaded with plane trees. Byzantine capitals, frescoes, and statues are scattered about a 16th-century altarpiece of the *Madonna and Saints* by Lorenzo Lotto and ceiling paintings by Veronese. ⏱ *30 min. Campo San Giacomo dell'Orio.* ☎ *041-2750462. Mon–Sat 10am–5pm; Sun 1–5pm. Vaporetto: Riva di Biasio.*

8 ★★ **Santa Maria e San Donato, Murano.** The exterior of the curved 12th-century apse is showily Byzantine and richly decorated with arches, balconies, and columns. Inside, the multicolored mosaics are reminiscent of those in San Marco. Most haunting is a mosaic figure of the Virgin who looks over the apse from a shining field of gold. ⏱ *30 min. Campo San Donato.* ☎ *041-739056. Mon–Sat 8:30am–noon, 4–7pm; Sun 4–6pm. Vaporetto: 12 from Fondamenta Nuove to Murano-Museo.*

9 ★★★ **Basilica di Santa Maria Assunta, Torcello.** The oldest building on the Venetian lagoon dates from the 7th century and once served a population of 20,000. Torcello was abandoned 1,000 years ago, but Byzantine splendors—the campanile, paintings, and mosaics—remain intact. The apse has a simple mosaic of a Madonna and Child, while at the other end of the church, a fear-invoking mosaic cycle portrays the Last Judgment—with lurid images of sinners burning as Lucifer watches. ⏱ *1 hr. Campo San Donato.* ☎ *041-730084. 3€. Apr–Oct daily 10:30am–5:30pm; Nov–Mar daily 10am–5pm. Vaporetto: 12 from Murano to Torcello.*

10 ★ **Santa Fosca, Torcello.** A pentagonal portico supported by elegant columns surrounds the small and sparsely elegant church built to house the body of Saint Fosca, brought to Torcello in the 11th century. ⏱ *30 min. Campo San Donato.* ☎ *041-739056. Apr–Oct daily 10:30am–5:30pm; Nov–Mar daily 10am–5pm. Vaporetto: Torcello.*

The church of San Giacomo dell'Orio.

Venice's Best Churches

1. Basilica di San Marco
2. San Zaccaria
3. San Francesco della Vigna
4. Santi Giovanni e Paolo
5. Santa Maria dei Miracoli
6. San Giacomo di Rialto
7. San Giacomo dall'Orio
8. Prosecco
9. San Zan Degolà
10. Santa Maria Gloriosa dei Frari
11. San Sebastiano
12. Santa Maria della Salute
13. Il Redentore
14. Hotel Cipriani
15. San Giorgio Maggiore
16. Santa Maria e San Donato
17. Basilica di Santa Maria Assunta

In Venice's churches—rebuilt over the centuries, lavishly decorated by generations of masters, and often painstakingly restored—the city's history and artistic heritage unfolds. Step into one, and the temptation to see the treasures housed in so many others will probably be irresistible. START: **Piazza San Marco**

1 ★★★ Basilica di San Marco. Venice merges its links to East and West in an arched, domed, and mosaic-paved Byzantine tour de force. ⏱ *2–3 hr. See p 23, bullet* **1**.

2 ★★ San Zaccaria. A glorious *Madonna and Child with Saints* by Giovanni Bellini lights up the interior of the Renaissance church that is dedicated to the father of John the Baptist. ⏱ *30 min. See p 57, bullet* **1**.

3 ★★ San Francesco della Vigna. One of the finest Renaissance churches in Venice has a 15th-century facade by Andrea Palladio, paintings by Veronese and Giovanni Bellini, and lovely cloisters. ⏱ *30 min. See p 58, bullet* **11**.

4 ★★ Santi Giovanni e Paolo. The largest Gothic church in Venice, a showy bastion of the Dominican order completed in 1430, is the unofficial pantheon of the doges. ⏱ *30 min. See p 58, bullet* **8**.

The church of San Zaccaria.

The church of San Giacomo di Rialto.

5 ★★★ Santa Maria dei Miracoli. Sheathed in white marble and perfectly proportioned, this Renaissance creation looks like an ornamental jewelry box. ⏱ *30 min. See p 66, bullet* **10**.

6 ★ San Giacomo di Rialto. The oldest church in Venice was founded in the 5th century and restored in the 11th century. ⏱ *1 hr. See p 23, bullet* **5**.

7 ★ San Giacomo dell'Orio. A distinctive ship's keel ceiling from 1225 shelters the apse, and ceiling paintings by Veronese decorate a chapel. ⏱ *30 min. See p 25, bullet* **7**.

Gondolas moored with Santa Maria della Salute in the background.

8 Prosecco. An equally well-known landmark on this square serves the namesake sparkling white as well as many other wines by the glass. *Campo San Giacomo dell'Orio, Santa Croce.* ☎ *041-5240222.*

9 ★★ San Zan Degolà. Recent restorations of this church have revealed simple but exquisite Byzantine frescoes. *Campo San Giovanni Decollato, Santa Croce. Vaporetto: San Basilio.*

10 ★★ Santa Maria Gloriosa dei Frari. The massive Italian

Gothic edifice is a treasure house of remarkable paintings and sculpture by Donatello, Bellini, and others. 🕐 *1 hr. See p 33, bullet* 10.

11 ★★ San Sebastiano. Paolo Veronese's fresco cycle and huge canvases pay tribute to the namesake saint. 🕐 *20 min. See p 32, bullet* 7.

12 ★★ Santa Maria della Salute. The glimmering white basilica stands guard over the entrance to the Grand Canal. Inside is Tineretto's *Wedding at Cana,* Titian's *St. Mark Enthroned with Saints,* and other treasures. 🕐 *30 min. See p 11, bullet* 1.

13 ★★★ Il Redentore. Built to assuage the plague of 1576, Andrea Palladio's graceful church is a stately presence on the islands of the Giudecca. 🕐 *2 hr. See p 46, bullet* 1.

14 Hotel Cipriani. Step from the sacred into the secular at the pool bar of this exclusive hideaway hotel, where you can sip a drink while ogling the swells lounging around the pool. *Fondamenta San Giovanni, Giudecca.* ☎ *041-5207744.*

The cloisters of San Giorgio Maggiore.

Santa Maria e San Donato, on the island of Murano.

⓯ ★★★ San Giorgio Maggiore.
An elegant church by architect
Andrea Palladio graces this island
directly across the lagoon from
San Marco. ⏱ *2 hr.* *See p 46, bullet ➋.*

**⓰ ★★ Santa Maria e San
Donato, Murano.** In the curved,
12th-century apse is a sea of multicolored mosaics. ⏱ *30 min.* *See p 25, bullet ➑.*

**⓱ ★★★ Basilica di Santa Maria
Assunta, Torcello.** The oldest
building on the Venetian lagoon is
adorned with a glorious, fearsome
mosaic cycle of *The Last Judgment.*
⏱ *1 hr.* *See p 25, bullet ➒.*

*A mosaic in the Basilica di Santa Maria
Assunta, on the island of Torcello.*

Master of Classicism

The most stately of Venice's churches are the work of Andrea
Palladio (1508–80), who was born in Padua and spent most of his life
in Venice. Perhaps the greatest architect of the Renaissance, Palladio
studied the ruins of ancient Rome and turned to the classical elements of symmetry, proportion, and harmony for the villas he built for
nobility on the mainland and the churches he designed in Venice. In
such churches as Il Redentore and San Giorgio Maggiore, look for the
telltale elements of Palladian style—tall columns, porticos like those
on Roman temples, and domes.

Best Places **to See Art**

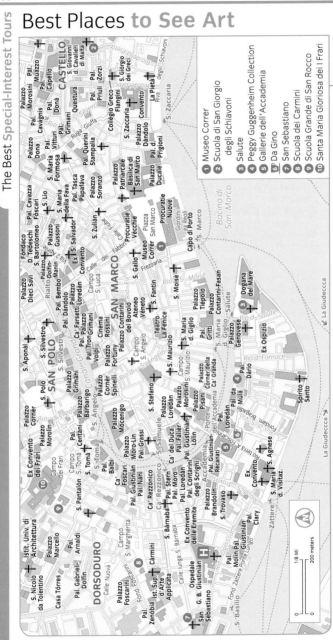

1. Museo Correr
2. Scuola di San Giorgio degli Schiavoni
3. Salute
4. Peggy Guggenheim Collection
5. Gallerie dell'Accademia
6. Da Gino
7. San Sebastiano
8. Scuola dei Carmini
9. Scuola Grande di San Rocco
10. Santa Maria Gloriosa dei l Frari

Can you actually see the great works of Venetian art in a day? If you're ambitious and pressed for time, yes. But it's hard to resist the temptation to linger for hours in any number of the city's fine museums and churches. If you're on a more leisurely trip, you can do this tour over the course of several days. START: **Piazza San Marco**

① ★ **Museo Correr.** The Museum of the City and Civilization of Venice provides some fascinating glimpses of Venetian life. In Carpaccio's *Two Venetian Ladies*, the bored subjects wait for their husbands to return from hunting. Among the other curiosities is a pair of sandals with 2-foot-tall heels upon which women of fashion once tottered. ⏱ *1 hr. Piazza San Marco.* ☎ *041-5225625. Apr–Oct daily 9am–7pm; Nov–Mar daily 9am–5pm.*

② ★★ **Scuola di San Giorgio degli Schiavoni.** Carpaccio spent 5 years painting his *Cycle of St. George*, an homage to the patron saints of the Slavic members of this *scuola* (guild). The painter's lush colors and flair for storytelling bring dragon-slaying to vivid life, detailed depictions of decomposing bodies, ferocious dragons, and out-of-body experiences may captivate you for hours. ⏱ *30 min. Calle dei Furlani.* ☎ *041-2750642. 3€. Apr–Oct Tues–Sat 9:30am– 12:30pm, 3:30–6:30pm, Sun 9:30am–12:30pm; Nov–Mar Tues–Sat 10am–12:30pm, 3–6pm, Sun 10am–12:30pm. Vaporetto: San Zaccaria.*

The Battle of Chioggia, *in the Museo Correr.*

③ ★★ **Salute.** Turn your back on the water views and walk up the majestic staircase of this baroque church to admire Tineretto's *Wedding at Cana*, Titian's *St. Mark Enthroned with Saints*, and other masterworks. ⏱ *30 min. See p 11, bullet* ①.

Carpaccio's Cycle of St. George, *in the Scuola di San Giorgio degli Schiavoni.*

Angel Playing the Lyre, by Carpaccio, in the Gallerie dell'Accademia.

4 ★★★ **Peggy Guggenheim Collection.** Picassos, Klees, and Miros hang in airy, light-filled galleries along the Grand Canal, all of it a refreshing antidote to the religious fervor that permeates most Venetian art. ⏲ 1 hr. See p 11, bullet **4**.

5 ★★★ **Gallerie dell'Accademia.** Three former religious buildings house the city's major art collection, a vast repository of Venetian art from the Byzantine to the rococo. A contemplation of just a few of the masterpieces here—Bellini's San Giobbi Altarpiece, Veronese's Supper in the House of Levi, and Titian's Pieta, for example—is an experience long remembered. ⏲ 2 hr. See p 34.

6 **Da Gino.** A handy stop near the Accademia serves delicious panini and hundreds of wines by the glass. Calle Nuova Sant'Agese, Dorsoduro. ☎ 041-5285276.

7 ★★ **San Sebastiano.** Paolo Veronese's frescoes of the church's namesake saint cover the walls, ceilings, even the organ doors. More striking than the saint's gruesome martyrdom, perhaps, is the artist's fascination with sumptuous colors and lavish costumes. ⏲ 30 min. Fondamenta di San Sebastiano.

☎ 041-2750642. 2€. Mon–Sat 10am–5pm; Sun 1–5pm. Vaporetto: San Basilio.

8 ★★ **Scuola dei Carmini.** In this remarkably well-preserved scuola founded by the Carmelites in the 17th century, one of Giambattista Tiepolo's great masterpieces, The Virgin in Glory Appearing to the Blessed Simon Stock, flows across the ceiling of the upper salon. Mirrors provided to view the painting help visitors capture the drama of the Virgin handing the saint a scapular, two pieces of cloth draped over the shoulders and worn as a sign of servitude. ⏲ 30 min. Campo dei Carmini. ☎ 041-5289420. 5€. Apr–Oct Mon–Sat 9am–6pm, Sun 9am–4pm; Nov–Mar daily 9am–4pm. Vaporetto: San Basilio.

9 ★★ **Scuola Grande di San Rocco.** Tintoretto was entrusted with decorating this school dedicated to the patron saint of the sick, and some of his greatest works are here. ⏲ 30 min. Campo San Rocco. ☎ 041-5234864. 5.50€. Apr–Oct daily 8am–12:30pm, 3–5pm; Nov–Mar

Titian's Assumption of the Virgin, in I Frari.

Mon–Fri 8am–12:30pm, Sat–Sun 8am–12:30pm, 2–4pm. Vaporetto: San Tomà.

⑩ ★★ Santa Maria Gloriosa dei Frari. By the time the massive Italian Gothic edifice was completed, around 1440 it was one of the largest churches in Venice; the campanile is the second highest on the lagoon, outstripped only by that of San Marco. The church is filled with remarkable paintings and sculpture.

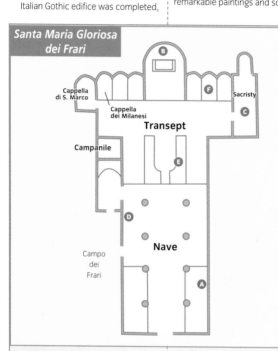

Santa Maria Gloriosa dei Frari

Cappella di S. Marco

Cappella dei Milanesi

Transept

Campanile

Nave

Campo dei Frari

Sacristy

Ⓐ Titian's tomb is a banal monument to the artist who bathed the church in bold colors. Titian succumbed to the plague in 1576 at age 90; the monument was put up 300 years later. In Titian's powerful rendition of the **Ⓑ Assumption of the Virgin,** Mary ascends from a crowd of awe-struck apostles amid a swirl of *putti* (cherubs). Giovanni Bellini's triptych **Ⓒ Madonna Enthroned with Saints** is filled with lute-playing angels. Titian painted **Ⓓ Madonna di Ca' Pesaro** in honor of Captain Jacopo Pesaro, whose papal fleet had just defeated the Turks. A refined Renaissance sculptural grouping, **Ⓔ Monuments to Doge Nicolò Tron and Doge Foscari,** rises above the tomb of Doge Tron. Foscari died of a broken heart when his son Jacopo was exiled in 1547. It's hard not to feel a pang of sympathy for **Ⓕ John the Baptist,** who in Donatello's amazingly lifelike rendering is decidedly scrawny and bedraggled. ⏱ *1 hr. Campo dei Frari. ☎ 041-5222637. 1.55€. Mon–Sat 9am 6pm; Sun 1–6pm. Vaporetto: San Tomà.*

The Accademia

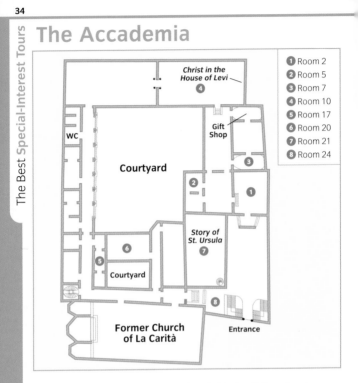

Christ in the
House of Levi

④

WC

Gift
Shop

Courtyard

②

①

③

Story of
St. Ursula

⑦

⑥

⑤

Courtyard

⑧

Former Church
of La Carità

Entrance

❶ Room 2
❷ Room 5
❸ Room 7
❹ Room 10
❺ Room 17
❻ Room 20
❼ Room 21
❽ Room 24

Venice's largest museum was founded in the 19th century to
house art from churches and convents suppressed by Napoleon.
Today's galleries occupy the monastery of the Lateran Canons, the
church of La Carità, and the Scuola Santa Maria della Carità. A visit is a
stroll through the great periods of Venetian art.

Room 2 Among eight magnificent
altarpieces is Giovanni Bellini's *Virgin
and Child with Saints*, often known
as the ★★★ *Pala di San Giobbe,*
for the Venetian church that commissioned the piece.

Room 5 The symbolism of ★★ *The
Tempest* by Giorgione, a portrayal of
a woman suckling her infant in an
eerie cast of green light, has evaded
scholars for centuries, adding to the
work's appealing mystery. The artist's
Old Woman, hanging nearby, evokes
the brevity of life—made all the more

poignant by the fact that the painter
died of the plague at age 35.

Room 7 Lorenzo Lotto's bold, stark
★★ *Portrait of a Young Gentle-
man in his Study* suggests that
moodiness, self-absorption, and
psychic unrest are not uniquely
modern-day preoccupations.

Room 10 Three great 16th-century
masters convene in one room.
Veronese painted his ★★ *Christ in
the House of Levi* as a *Last
Supper,* but church authorities
found the ribaldry and Venetian

setting heretical, so he changed the name. Titian, at 90, painted the *Pieta* for his tomb but died before finishing it. Tintoretto's ★★ **St. Mark cycle** includes some of his finest works, illustrating, among other moments, the theft of the saint's body.

Room 17 Canaletto's views of the Grand Canal, Francesco Guardi's *Isola di San Giorgio,* and other pleasant 18th-century Venetian scenes may be familiar. What you may not have seen before are the works of a female artist, Rosalba Carriera.

Room 20 In the 15th and 16th centuries, the Scuola di San Giovanni Evangelista commissioned Venetian painters to illustrate *Miracles of the Relic of the True Cross*. Carpaccio's effort is a fascinating detailed look at Venice in that distant past, when a wooden bridge crossed the Grand Canal at the Rialto.

Room 21 Carpaccio's ★★ *Story of Saint Ursula* is a color-saturated, action-packed medieval travelogue in which the Breton princess and her English betrothed, Hereus,

Portrait of a Young Man *(Memling).*

travel to Rome so the groom-to-be can be converted to the true faith.

Room 24 Titian painted his *Presentation of the Virgin to the Temple* for this room, the former *albergo* of the Scuola della Carità. This elegant rendering is a graceful endnote to our visit. ⏱ *2–3 hr. Campo Carità.* ☎ *041-5222247.* € *6.50. Mon 8:15am–2pm; Tues–Sun 8:15am– 7:15pm. Vaporetto: Accademia.*

Arrival of the English Ambassadors *(Carpaccio).*

The Best Special-Interest Tours

Great Venetian Palazzi **to Visit**

0 ____ 1/8 Mi

0 ____ 200 meters

CANNAREGIO

Scuola dei Mercanti
Madonna dell'Orto
Casino dei Spiriti
Pal. Arrigoni
Pal. Mastelli
Pal. Contarini dal Zaffo
Casa di Tintoretto
Sacca della Misericordia

Sinagoghe (Museo Ebráico)
GHETTO
Rio terrà S. Leonardo
Ex Convento S. M. dei Servi
Cappella d. Volto Santo
S. Marziale
Scuola Vécchia d. Misericordia
S. Maria d. Misericordia
Ex Convento e Chiesa di S. Caterina
Gesuiti
Pal. Donà
Fond. Nove

Pal. Labia
S. Marcuola
S. Geremia
Riva da Biásio
La Maddalena
Pal. Lezze
Pal. Vendramin
Pal. Papafava
Ex Convento
Pal. Seriman

Pal. Marcello-Toderini
Fónd. d. Turchi
Ca' Tron
S. Stae
Pal. Erizzo
Pal. Molin
S. Marcuola
S. Felice
Ca' d'Oro
S. Sofia
Ss. Apóstoli
S. Canciano
Pal. Widman

S. Zan Degolà
Palazzo Mocenigo
Ca' Pesaro
S. Maria Máter Domini
Palazzo Brandolin
Ca' d'Oro
Pal. Mangilli
Ca' da Mosto
Pal. Grifalconi

SANTA CROCE
S. Giacomo dell'Orio
Pal. Zane
Pal. Grioni
S. Cassiano
Pescaria
Ca' da Mosto
Pal. Civran
Teatro Málibran
Pal. Soranzo-Van Axel

Pal. Zane Collalto
Pal. Muti Baglioni
Fábbriche Nuove

Ex Convento dei Frari
Palazzo Morolin
Campo S. Polo
S. Polo
Palazzo Dieci Savi
Ponte di Rialto
Rialto
Fóndaco D Tedeschi
S. Bartolomeo
Pal. Marcelo Pindemonte
Palazzo Dona

R. terrà S. Tomà
Campo dei Frari
S. Maria G. dei Frari
S. Tomà
Pal. Centani
S. Silvestro
S. Silvestro
Palazzo Grimani
Pal. Dándolo
Ca' Farsetti
Loredán
Palazzo Dolfin-Manin
Pal. Gussoni
S. Salvador
Ex Convento
S. Maria Formosa
Pal. Tasca Papafáva

Pal. Balbi
Ca' Foscari
S. Tomà
Pal. Mocenigo
Pal. Volpi
Cinema Rossini
SAN MARCO
S. Zuliàn
Palazzo Soranzo
Palazzo Patriarcale

Palazzo Moro-Lin
Pal. Grassi
Palazzo Cornèr Spinelli
Campo S. Ángelo
Ateneo Véneto
Pal. Contarini del Bovolo
S. Gallo
Procuratie Vécchie
Basilica di San Marco

Pal. Nani
S. Samuele
Ca' Rezzonico
Palazzo Loredàn
S. Stefano
Teatro La Fenice
S. Fantin
Museo Correr
Piazza San Marco
Pal. d. Prigioni

Pal. Moro
Ca' del Dúca
Pal. Falièr
Pal. Bárbaro
Palazzo Pisani
Palazzo Morosini
S. Maurizio
S. Maria d. Giglio
S. Moisè
Procuratie Nuove
Palazzo Ducale

Accademia
Ca' Rezzonico
Palazzo Cornèr della Ca' Granda
Pal. Gritti
Pal. Ferro Fini
Palazzo Giustinián
Palazzo Tiépolo
S. Marco
Giardini ex Reali

Gallerie dell'Accademia
Ponte dell'Accademia
S. Maria d. Giglio-Salute
Pal. Genovese
Dogana da Mar
Bacino di San Marco

S. Maria d. Visitáz.
S. Agnese
Gesuati
Pal. Venier dei Leoni (Guggenheim)
S. Maria d. Salute
Ex Ospizio

Záttere
Spirito Santo
Fond. Záttere ai Saloni

Canale della Giudecca

Palanca
Fónd. S. Giacomo

Ísola della Giudecca
Redentore
Il Redentore
Ex Chiesa della Croce

1 Palazzo Ducale
2 Museo della Fondazione Querini Stampalia
3 Palazzo Fortuny
4 Palazzo Cini
5 Ca' Rezzonico/Museo del Settecento Veneziano
6 Ca' Pesaro/Museo d'Arte Orientale and Galleria Internazionale d'Arte Moderna
7 Da Baffo
8 Ca' d'Oro/Galleria Franchetti

Venetian nobility began building elaborate palaces as early as the 1st century, and the best address, or course, was the Grand Canal. None of the residences built along this busy waterway or elsewhere in the city were known as palaces—the term *palazzo* was reserved for the home and headquarters of the doge. Many of these palazzi now house exquisite collections of art, making a visit doubly rewarding. START: **Piazza San Marco**

① ★★★ Palazzo Ducale. Doges ruled the Venetian Republic from this suitably grandiose palace, built and rebuilt many times from the 7th to the 18th centuries. It's a testament to the stability of the state that the palace was not a castle or fortress, but an elegant assemblage of pink and white marble. The facade is punctuated with sculpted figures representing wisdom and other virtues, and the 18 pointed archways are not just decorative: The doges witnessed public executions from the central arch. See p 38.

② ★ Museo della Fondazione Querini Stampalia. Giovanni Querini, a 19th-century scientist, bequeathed his family palazzo and fabulous art to the city of Venice, with the proviso that the premises remain open in the evening. The recently renovated galleries are still the late-night place to see enticing scenes of Venetian life by Pietro Longhi and Giovanni Bellini, as well as contemporary works. ⏱ *45 min. Campo Santa Maria Formosa.* ☎ *041-2711411.*

www.querinistampalia.it. Museum: 6€. Library: Free. Museum: Tues– Thurs and Sun 10am–10pm; Fri–Sat 10am–10pm. Library: Mon–Fri 4pm– midnight; Sat 2:30pm–midnight; Sun 3–7pm. Vaporetto: Rialto.

③ ★ Palazzo Fortuny. Mariano Fortuny (1871–1949), the Spanish artist and textile designer, bought and restored this 15th-century palazzo. The exotic fashions he created for the rich and famous using medieval dyeing and threading techniques are now on display in the salons. ⏱ *1 hr. Campo San Beneto.* ☎ *041-2747607. 4€. Tues–Sun 10am–6pm. Vaporetto: San Angelo.*

④ ★★ Palazzo Cini. A collector's eye is much in evidence in the home of industrialist Vittorio Cini (1885-1977), who filled the rooms with religious works by Sandro Botticelli, Piero della Francesca, and other Tuscan painters. ⏱ *45 min. Campo Carità.* ☎ *041-5222247. 6.50€. Mon 8:15am–2pm; Tues–Sun 8:15am– 7:15pm. Vaporetto: Accademia.*

The dungeon in the Palazzo Ducale.

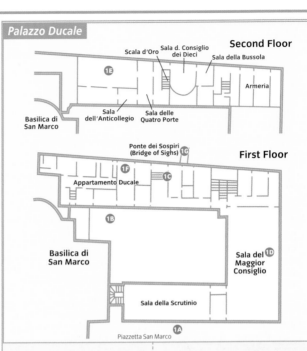

Palazzo Ducale

Second Floor

Scala d'Oro
Sala d. Consiglio dei Dieci
Sala della Bussola
Armeria
Basilica di San Marco
Sala dell'Anticollegio
Sala delle Quatro Porte

First Floor

Ponte dei Sospiri (Bridge of Sighs)
Appartamento Ducale
Basilica di San Marco
Sala del Maggior Consiglio
Sala della Scrutinio
Piazzetta San Marco

1A Porta della Carta, an elaborate archway of pink marble, is named for the edicts once posted here and graced with the two ubiquitous symbols of Venice: Saint Mark and the winged lion. In the courtyard beyond, the **1B Giant's Staircase** is flanked by statues of Mars and Neptune; doges were sworn in at the top. **1C Scala d'Oro,** the Golden Staircase, was designed by 16th-century classicist Sansovino to impress visiting dignitaries. It ascends beneath a 24-carat gold leaf ceiling. The Grand Council met in the vast **1D Sala del Maggior Consiglio** to appoint holders of public office and to elect new doges. Portraits of 76 of these officials line the walls beneath a ceiling painting of *Paradise* by Jacopo and Domenico Tintoretto;

a likeness of doge Marino Faller, beheaded in the 14th century for betraying the senate, is painted over. In the **1E Sala dei Senato,** nobles debated state affairs as the doge looked on from his throne. The **1F Sala dello Scudo** houses the globes and maps that enabled officials to keep track of trade routes and the discoveries of Marco Polo and other explorers. Much-romanticized but quite utilitarian, the **1G Ponte dei Sospiri** links the palace with a 17th-century prison (see p 48). 🕐 *1 hr. Piazzetta San Marco.* 📞 *041-5224951. 14€ (includes Museo Correr). Nov–Mar daily 9am–5pm; Apr–Oct daily 9am–7pm. Vaporetto: San Marco/ Vallaresso.*

Ca' Rezzonico.

international Modernist crowd are well represented, too. 🕐 *1 hr.* ☎ *041-5240662. 5.50€, Apr–Oct Tues–Sun 10am–6pm; Nov–Mar Tues–Sun 10am–5pm. Vaporetto: San Stae.*

7️⃣ Da Baffo. One of the best lunch spots in this part of town serves salads as well as heartier pasta dishes. *Campo Sant'Agostin, San Polo.* ☎ *041-5208862.*

5️⃣ ★★ Ca' Rezzonico/Museo del Settecento Veneziano. In the onetime home of poets Robert Browning and Elizabeth Barrett Browning, sweeping staircases and flamboyant salons are the backdrop for 18th-century artworks that include views of the Grand Canal by Canaletto and Pietro Longhi's scenes of everyday Venetian life. 🕐 *1 hr. Fondamenta Rezzonico.* ☎ *041-2410100. 6.50€. Wed–Tues 10am–6pm. Vaporetto: Ca' Rezzonico.*

6️⃣ ★ Ca' Pesaro/Museo d'Arte Orientale and Galleria Internazionale di Arte Moderna. In 1628, the illustrious Pesaro family (who appear with so little humility next to the Madonna in Titian's *Madonna di Ca' Pesaro* in the Frari; see p 33), commissioned architect Baldassare Longhena to combine three Gothic houses to create one of Venice's largest palaces. The elaborate surroundings now house the **Museo d'Arte Orientale** and the **Galleria Internazionale di Arte Moderna.** Swords, puppets, and other paraphernalia from Japan in the Oriental galleries were the passion of a 19th-century Venetian count/ collector. Many of the works in the modern galleries are by De Chirico, Morandi, and other Italians. Chagall, Klimt, Klee, Miró, and the rest of the

8️⃣ ★ Ca' d'Oro/Galleria Franchetti. The golden facade that gave this palace its name has faded, but plenty of treasures remain within, where a mosaic-paved entryway, a marble wellhead in the courtyard, and a second-floor balcony overlooking the Grand Canal provide a glimpse of the lifestyle of Renaissance nobility. *Saint Sebastian,* by Andrea Mantegna, the artist's last painting, is often considered his best. A transcendent *Annunciation* by Carpaccio and works by other masters such as Tintoretto, Signorelli, Titian, and Guardi make a good showing, too. 🕐 *1 hr.* ☎ *041-5200345. 5€. Mon 8:15am–4pm; Tues–Sun 8:15am–7:15pm. Vaporetto: Ca d'Oro.*

Portrait of a Priest *(Carena), in the Museo d'Arte Moderna di Ca' Pesaro.*

Venice's **Best Campos**

1. Piazza San Marco
2. Campiello dei Remer
3. Campo della Maddalena
4. Campo Santi Giovanni e
   San Paolo (San Zanipòlo)
5. The Rialto
6. All'Arco
7. Campo San Polo
8. Campo Santa Margherita
9. Pizzeria al Sportivi
10. Campo San Barnaba

Outdoor life in Venice is a social enterprise, often transpiring in a lively campo. A church or two, a few palazzi, a cafe, a row of market stalls, a nearby canal are the backdrops for these outdoor stages, and scenes of Venetian life are the show. START: **Piazza San Marco**

① ★★★ Piazza San Marco.

The only square in Venice to be known as a piazza rather than a campo is referred to simply as "the Piazza." Napoleon called the square the "finest drawing room in Europe," evoking San Marco's air of civility and sophistication as well as its raison d'être: It's a place for Venetians and their visitors to rub shoulders, drink coffee, and gawk for the first or the thousandth time at the exotic arches and domes. ⏱ *30 min. Vaporetto: San Marco/Vallaresso.*

② ★ Campiello dei Remer.

No small part of this little square's charm is the Grand Canal, lapping up against one side of the pavement. Byzantine arches gracing an adjoining palazzo and an ornately decorated well supply a picturesque

Orchestra playing in the Piazza San Marco.

Verrocchio's equestrian statue in the Campo Santi Giovanni e San Paolo.

backdrop for the colorful flotilla ever-present on the canal. ⏱ *15 min. Vaporetto: Rialto.*

③ ★ Campo della Maddalena.

Small houses topped with fantastically shaped chimney pots and a round, canal-side church lend an exotic air to this backwater corner where little has changed since the Middle Ages. ⏱ *15 min. Vaporetto: Ca' d'Oro.*

④ ★★★ Campo Santi Giovanni e San Paolo (San Zanipòlo).

There's an amiable bustle of activity around the massive basilica, the medieval Scuola Grande di San Marco, and Verrocchio's equestrian statue of Bartolomeo Colleoni. ⏱ *15 min. Fondamenta Nuove.*

5 ★★ **The Rialto.** Squares along the Grand Canal accommodate the hustle, bustle, and everyday business around the Ponte di Rialto. Fishmongers, businesspeople, housewives, and, of course, the ubiquitous sightseers congregate in markets and along narrow alleys. The scene may not be that different today than it was as long ago as the 5th century.

6 **All'Arco**. Almost as much a part of the Rialto as the markets, this old-fashion *bacaro* (wine bar) serves tasty *cicheti* (bar snacks). *Calle dell'Ochialer, San Polo.* ☎ *041-5205666.*

7 ★★ **Campo San Polo.** *Bull Baiting in the Campo San Polo,* a17th-century painting by German artist Joseph Heintz hanging in the Museo Correr (see p 31), provides a telling glimpse of the colorful past of this large square, still the lively heart of its namesake neighborhood. These days the top crowd-drawing spectacle is a summertime outdoor cinema, though the neighborhood comings and goings provide an amusing show at any time. ⏱ *15 min. Vaporetto: San Tomà.*

8 ★★★ **Campo Santa Margherita.** Two churches and two *scuoli* share this welcoming square with cafes, market stalls, and, on a fine day, what seems to be most of the population of Venice stealing a few moments in the sun. The eponymous saint, patron of expectant mothers, is remembered twice: A dragon, her symbol, embellishes a niche on the north end, and another decorates the base of the truncated campanile of her namesake church. ⏱ *30 min. Vaporetto: Ca' Rezzonico.*

9 **Pizzeria al Sportivi.** A chance to sit and watch the comings and goings on one of Venice's liveliest squares is just part of the appeal of this ever-busy spot—the pizza is also among the best in Venice. *Campo Santo Margherita.* ☎ *041-5211598.*

10 ★★ **Campo San Barnaba.** Nothing about this little square is what might be termed spectacular, but even a brief walk across its old paving stones is likely to be memorable. The 14th-century campanile of the namesake church rises above the small houses; a boat moored alongside a quay serves as the neighborhood greengrocer; and just downstream is the picturesquely arched Ponte dei Pugni (Bridge of the Punches), where rival clans once slugged out their differences. ⏱ *15 min. Vaporetto: Ca' Rezzonico.*

Floating greengrocer moored along the quay near the Campo San Barnaba.

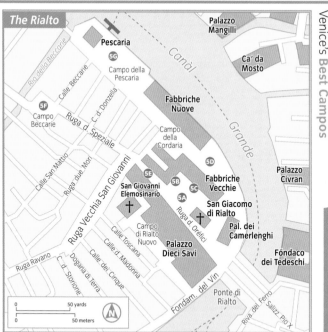

The Rialto

Palazzo Mangilli
Pescaria
5G
Campo della Pescaria
Ca' da Mosto
Canàl
Rio della Beccarie
Calle Beccarie
5F
Campo Beccarie
Ruga d. Speziale
C. d. Donzella
Fabbriche Nuove
Campo della Cordaria
Grande
Calle San Mattio
Ruga due Mori
Ruga Vecchia San Giovanni
5E
San Giovanni Elemosinario
5B
5D
Fabbriche Vecchie
Palazzo Civran
5C
5A
San Giacomo di Rialto
Ruga d. Orefici
Campo di Rialto Nuovo
Calle Toscana
Calle d. Madonna
Palazzo Dieci Savi
Pal. dei Camerlenghi
Ruga Ravano
C. d. Storione
Dogana di Terra
Calle dei Cinque
Fóndaco dei Tedeschi
Fondam. del Vin
Ponte di Rialto
Riva del Ferro
Salizz. Pio X

0 50 yards
0 50 meters

5A **Campo San Giacomo di Rialto** is a sea of fruit and vegetable stalls, above which rise the facade and campanile of the oldest church in Venice, founded the same year as the city, 421. The present structure dates to the 11th century. **5B** **The Gobbo di Rialto,** the "Hunchback of the Rialto," crouches on one side of the campo beneath a rostrum from which proclamations were read. For some Venetians, the humble figure was a welcome sight—he marked the end of a "walk of shame" that those found guilty of petty crimes were forced to make naked from San Marco. **5C** **Calle de Banco Giro** is a covered passageway that may have been the world's first banking premises: Merchants and moneylenders once gathered here to take advantage of the city's "giro" system, a paperless transfer of funds from one

party to another. In **5D** **Campo Erberia** stalls piled high with fresh fruit and vegetables stand in the shadow of the Fabbriche Nuove and the Fabbriche Vecchie, 16th-century warehouses. **5E** **Ruga degli Orefici,** the "Passageway of the Goldsmiths," still houses a few shops selling gold and silver, as it has since the 14th century. In **5F** **Campo Beccarie,** market stalls selling meat maintain a long-standing tradition— the city's abattoir once stood here. In **5G** **Campo della Pescaria,** the porticos of a neo-Gothic hall shelter a daily fish market. Alleyways leading off the square likewise bear the telltale names of the tradesmen who once set up shop in the environs (*Casaria,* or Cheese) and of the taverns that served them (*Due Mori,* The Two Moors). 🕐 *30 min. Vaporetto: Rialto.*

Venice's Most Memorable Views

1. The Piazzetta.
2. Campanile, San Marco
3. Harry's Bar
4. Ponte di Rialto
5. Punta della Dogana
6. San Giorgio Maggiore
7. Torcello

Venice is the most whimsical of places, and the play of sky, water, and marble is all the more transporting from any of the city's viewpoints. START: **Piazza San Marco**

---

1 ★ The Piazzetta. No other Venetian view imparts a greater sense of the city as a maritime republic. Two columns (one dedicated to San Marco, one to San Teodoro, the city's other patron saint) frame a flotilla of gondolas and the shimmering waters of the lagoon. Rising out of a sea mist are the domes and towers of Salute, San Giorgio, Redentore, and many other great monuments of Venice. ⏱ *15 min. Vaporetto: San Marco/Vallaresso.*

2 ★★ Campanile, San Marco. A bell tower has risen above the Piazza San Marco since the 10th century—with the exception of a decade in the early 20th century, when the brick structure by Renaissance master Bertola Bon collapsed without warning on July 14, 1902. The expansive outlook over the city, the sea, and the countryside all the way north to the Alps was restored with the completion of a new tower in 1912. ⏱ *1 hr. (or longer, depending on wait).* ☎ *041-5224064. 6€.*

Apr–Sept daily 9:30am–dusk; Oct–Mar daily 9:30am–3:30pm. Vaporetto: San Marco/Vallaresso.

3 **Harry's Bar.** Set your sights on celebrities and partake of another Venetian institution: a Bellini, the fresh peach juice/sparkling wine combination that was invented on these hallowed premises. *Calle Vallaresso, San Marco.* ☎ *041-5285777.*

4 ★★ **Ponte di Rialto.** A nonstop water show takes place beneath the most monumental of the spans across the Grand Canal: Gondolas, garbage scows, police launches, and all manner of other craft ply the crowded waterway. Also in close view: the centuries-old commercial heart of the city, the **Fondaco dei Tedeschi**, built in 1508 as a warehouse and now the city's main post office; the **Palazzo dei Camerlenghi**, built in 1525 and the world's first-known office building; and two of the city's first palaces, the **Palazzo Loredan** and

Palazzo Farsetti, which now jointly house city hall. ⏱ *30 min. Vaporetto: Rialto.*

5 ★★ **Punta della Dogana.** From the Customs house at the tip of the Dorsoduro, San Marco glimmers across the basin. Straight ahead are the sea lanes that seduced so many traders and explorers. ⏱ *15 min. Vaporetto: Salute.*

6 ★★★ **San Giorgio Maggiore.** The view from the island's campanile is even more expansive than that from the campanile in San Marco, and there's no wait to ascend. ⏱ *30 min. See p 46, bullet* **2**.

7 ★★ **Torcello.** The highest point on the island of the "little tower" is the 12th-century campanile of the cathedral. A ramp twists to the top, and from here Venice appears as a phantom city across the waters of the lagoon. ⏱ *30 min.* ☎ *041-2702464. 2€. Apr–Oct daily 10:30am–5:30pm; Nov–Mar daily 10am–4:45pm. Vaporetto: Torcello.*

View from the Campanile in Piazza San Marco.

Places to **Escape the Crowds**

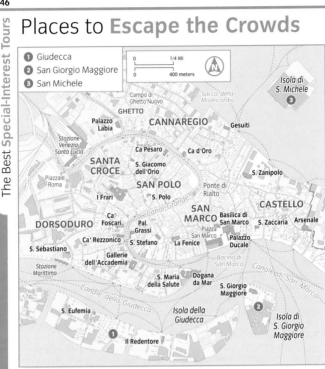

1 Giudecca
2 San Giorgio Maggiore
3 San Michele

I n Venice, an island escape is only a short vaporetto ride away, and the retreat usually comes with a nice smattering of art and architecture. START: **Vaporetto 41, 42, or 82 to Zitelle**

1 ★★ **Giudecca.** Once a bucolic getaway for wealthy Venetians, this string of eight connected islands still seems far removed from the bustle of the city. Walks through quiet neighborhoods and visits to three famous churches are the pastimes here. **Il Redentore,** the grandest, was begun as an offering to the Redeemer in the midst of a plague outbreak, in 1576. More than a third of the city succumbed to the disease, but work on the church continued for two decades, and it's now an elegant showcase for the restrained classicism of architect Andrea

Palladio. **La Zitelle,** "church of the spinsters," is so-named because young women whose families could not afford a dowry were once sent to the adjoining convent to learn lace making. The church of **Santa Eufemia** is much older than its Palladian neighbors. It was founded in the 9th century and rebuilt in the 11th century to a Byzantine design. ⏲ *2 hr. Il Redentore: 2€.* ☎ *041-2750642. Mon–Sat 10am–5pm; Sun 1–5pm. Vaporetto: Redentore.*

2 ★★★ **San Giorgio Maggiore.** Benedictine monks have inhabited this island directly across the lagoon from San Marco for more than 1,000 years. They still impose a veil of tranquillity on a stunning complex that includes a church by Andrea Palladio, two cloisters, and a bell tower that affords heart-stopping views over the city and its surroundings (see p 45). The Fondazione Cini, founded by industrialist Vittorio Cini to support cultural causes, shares the premises with a small community of monks and occasionally hosts conferences and art exhibitions. ⏲ *2 hr.* ☎ *041-5227827. Campanile: 3€. Apr–Sept Mon–Sat 9am–12:30pm, 2:30–6:30pm, Sun 9:30–10:30am, 2:30–6:30pm; Oct–Mar daily 9:30am–12:30pm, 2:30–5pm. Vaporetto: San Giorgio.*

③ ★★ **San Michele.** The last stop for many Venetians is the cypress-studded island that has served as the city cemetery since the late 18th century, when the city imposed a ban on burying the dead in the water-soaked earth around churches. San Michele is the resting place of many distinguished expatriates—among them, Ezra Pound, Igor Stravinsky, and Serge Diaghilev,

A gondola floats across the lagoon, with San Giorgio Maggiore in the background.

whose grave is usually strewn with dance slippers. Gondoliers are as lively a presence in death as they were in life, and lie beneath elaborately carved models of the craft they so deftly maneuvered. Venice's first Renaissance church, **San Michele in Isola,** stands alongside the lagoon at the entrance to this enchanting island of the dead. ⏲ *1 hr. Apr–Sept daily 7:30am–6pm; Oct–Mar daily 7:30am–4pm. Vaporetto: Cimitero.*

Dancer Serge Diaghilev's grave, strewn with flowers and ballet slippers, in the San Michele Cemetery.

Venice's Most Photogenic Ponti

1. Bridge of Sighs
2. Ponte di Rialto
3. Ponte Chiodo
4. Il Gelatone
5. Ponte dei Tre Archi

The humorist Robert Benchley once sent a telegram to his editor from Venice, "Streets full of water. Please advise." The response may well have been to make use of the 400 bridges that cross Venice's waterways. That number will increase with the much-anticipated opening of a fourth span across the Grand Canal, designed by the acclaimed Spanish architect Santiago Calatrava. START: **Riva degli Schiavoni**

1 ★★ Bridge of Sighs. Legend has it that Venice's second-most famous bridge takes its name from the sighs of prisoners stealing their last glimpses of freedom as they made their way to dank cells or the executioner's block. Travelers as savvy as Mark Twain have fallen for the story (he said the bridge led to "the dungeon which none entered and hoped to see the sun again"), but it's bunk. The handsome span,

nicely viewed from the Riva degli Schiavoni, connects the Palazzo Ducale with a prison constructed in the late 16th century to house petty criminals, just about all of whom saw the light of day again. ⏱ *15 min. Vaporetto: San Zaccaria.*

2 ★★★ Ponte di Rialto. This famous, shop-lined marble span, designed by the aptly named A. Ponte, dates from 1590. For a long time it was the only bridge across the Grand Canal. Today, it's a favorite of souvenir hawkers and tourists. A bridge of boats crossed this narrow stretch of the Grand Canal until the 13th century, when a succession of wooden bridges went up—an especially scenic one appears in Carpaccio's *The Miracle of the True Cross* in the Accademia (see p 34). 🕐 *15 min. Vaporetto: Rialto.*

3 ★ Ponte Chiodo. One of Venice's two remaining bridges with no parapets crosses a canal in a quiet corner of the Castello. The other one, the Ponte del Diavolo, is on the island of Torcello (see p 45). 🕐 *15 min. Vaporetto: Ca' d'Oro.*

4 Il Gelatone. The reward for a trek into the far reaches of the Cannaregio neighborhood is a scoop of gelato from this much-admired provider. *Rio Terrà Maddalena, Cannaregio.* ☎ *041-720631.*

Sculpture on the Rialto Bridge.

5 ★ Ponte dei Tre Archi. Venice's only three-arched bridge crosses the Cannaregio Canal in a series of steps. Engineer Andrea Tirali, known by his work crew as "Il Tiranno" (the tyrant), completed the elegant span in 1688. The view from the bridge is rewarding; a parade of boats plies the busy waterway. 🕐 *15 min. Vaporetto: Ponte Tre Archi.*

The Bridge of Sighs in the morning mist.

Best Places to Explore Venetian Craftsmanship

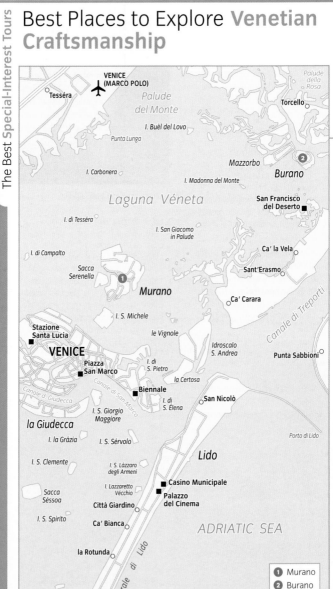

VENICE
(MARCO POLO)

Tesséra

Palude del Monte

Palude della Rosa

Torcello

I. Buèl del Lovo

Punta Lunga

I. Carbonera

Mazzorbo

Burano ❷

I. Madonna del Monte

Laguna Véneta

San Francisco del Deserto ■

I. di Tesséra

I. San Giacomo in Palude

I. di Campalto

Sacca Serenella

❶

Ca' la Vela

Sant'Erasmo

Murano

Ca' Carara

Canale di Treporti

I. S. Michele

le Vignole

Stazione Santa Lucia ■

Idroscalo S. Andrea

VENICE

Piazza San Marco ■

I. di S. Pietro

la Certosa

Punta Sabbioni

Biennale ■

I. di S. Élena

San Nicolò

Canale d. Giudecca

Canale di San Marco

I. S. Giorgio Maggiore

la Giudecca

I. la Grázia

I. S. Sérvolo

Porto di Lido

I. S. Clemente

I. S. Lázzaro degli Armeni

Lido

Sacca Séssoa

I. Lazzaretto Vécchio

Casino Municipale ■

I. S. Spirito

Città Giardino

Palazzo del Cinema ■

Ca' Bianca

ADRIATIC SEA

la Rotunda

Litorale di Lido

I. Povéglia

Malamocco

Instituto Marino San Marco ■

❶ Murano
❷ Burano

0   1 Mi
0   2 Km

Glassmakers emigrated to Venice in great numbers after the fall of Constantinople in 1292. By the 16th century glassworks had been relegated to the island of Murano as a measure to prevent fire from raging through the city. Since then, Murano has become synonymous with glass. Meanwhile, lace making has occupied many of the inhabitants of Burano for centuries. A visit to both islands is an introduction to ages-old Venetian craftsmanship.

START: **Vaporetto no. 12 from Fondamenta Nuove to Murano (Colonna stop), continuing to Burano**

1 ★★ Murano. The glassmakers' island is not always mellow, especially when shills swoop upon passengers disembarking from the vaporetto like pigeons on bread crumbs in San Marco and try to whisk them off to studios and shops along the Fondamenta dei Vetrai. Even so, many of the glass pieces fashioned in the island furnaces are temptingly attractive. For those who seek a respite from shopping, two beautiful churches provide welcome refuge. See p 52.

2 ★★ Burano. The most cheerful patch of land in the lagoon is home to lace makers and fishermen. Houses are painted in bright colors, allegedly so they can be spotted from boats at sea. A pleasant scene unfolds on almost any street on the island, where women fashion pieces

A glass blower in a Murano factory.

The island of Murano, with Santa Maria e San Donato church.

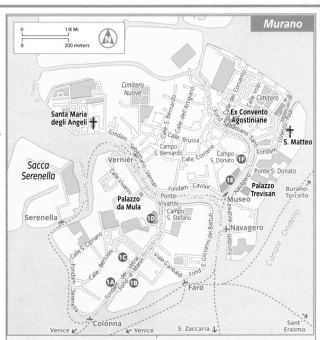

Murano

Many of the establishments offering Murano glass along the **1A ★ Fondamenta dei Vetrai** and those nearby are reputable and sell lovely wares but are best visited without the company of a high-pressure guide. **1B L'Arte Muranese** *(Fondamenta Manin 61;* ☎ *041-73914)* offers a fine selection of antique and modern glass in a pleasantly low-key setting. **1C Fratelli Barbini** *(Calle Bertolini 36, 041 739 777)*, one of the island's most respected glass houses, welcomes guests to its glass-blowing studios and offers its enticing wares at factory prices. In **1D ★ San Pietro Martire**, chandeliers fashioned in Murano's glass furnaces illuminate paintings of Saint Jerome and Saint Agatha by Veronese, as well as works by such masters as Tintoretto, Bellini, and Titian. *Fondamenta dei Vetrai.*

☎ *041-739704.* **1E ★★ Museo dell'Arte Vetraria,** in an old palazzo, displays pieces from ancient Rome and those made on Murano during the Middle Ages and Renaissance, as well as some stunning modern Murano glass. 🕐 *1 hr. Piazza Galuppi 181. 4€* ☎ *041-739586. Thurs–Tues 10am–5pm (until 4pm Nov–Mar).* Dating to the seventh century and rebuilt in the 12th century, **1F ★★ Santa Maria e San Donato** is one of the most splendid Byzantine structures on the lagoon, its floor glittering with mosaics. Look for the mosaic figure of the Virgin, who looks over the apse from a glittering field of gold. The eerie-looking objects behind the altar are bones, said to be those of the dragon slain by Saint Donato. See p 25, bullet 8.

of lace in the doorways and men mend fishing nets. The island's lively gathering spots are Piazza Galuppi and the fish market along Fondamenta Pescheria. Burano has been known for its lace making since the 15th century, when young women in Venice and the islands on the lagoon were encouraged to learn the craft—a genteel pastime, and a lucrative export business. By the 18th century, lace manufacture, and many Venetian lace makers along with it, had shifted to France. Burano is credited with reinvigorating the art with its lace-making school, Scuola di Merletti, founded in 1872 to train new generations in such distinctive stitches as Burano point. See p 54.

The charming island of Burano.

3 Al Gatto Nero. A delicious lunch of fresh fish or seafood pasta comes, appropriately, with a view of the commotion at Burano's fish market across the canal. *Fondamenta della Giudecca 88, Burano.* ☎ *041-730120.*

An example of the lace of Burano.

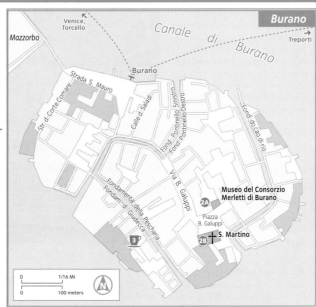

Burano's lace-making Scuola di Merletti has few followers these days, but the museum, **2A** ★★ **Museo del Consorzio Merletti di Burano,** houses a collection of handkerchiefs, collars, napkins, altar cloths, and other items made in intricate lace patterns. ⏱ *1 hr. Piazza B. Galuppi 181. 4€.* ☎ *041-730034. Wed–Mon 10am–5pm.* The romantically leaning campanile and simple brick facade of **2B** ★ **San Martino** face Piazza Baldassarre Galuppi, named for the island-born composer of opera buffa. A Crucifixion by Tiepolo hangs in the left aisle, near a large stone sarcophagus that legend says was dragged ashore by saints Alban, Dominic, and Orso and island children; a charming painting depicts the event. The presence of the three saints, who are interred in the altar, allegedly saved the island from the devastating plague outbreak of 1630. ⏱ *30 min. Piazza Galuppi. Daily 8am–noon, 3–7pm.* ●

A lacemaker on Burano.

Castello & Sant'Elena

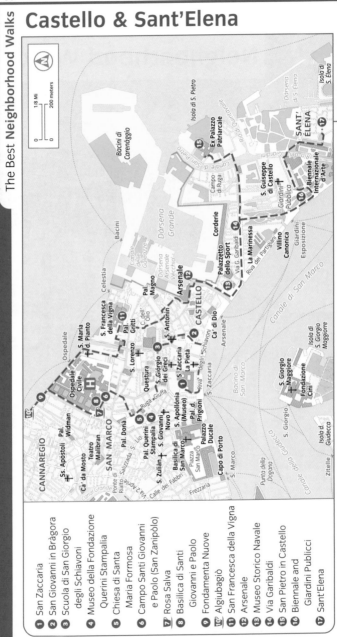

Coming upon colorful scenes of everyday Venetian life is one of the great pleasures of wandering though this large neighborhood, which stretches from the Rialto east to the island enclave of Sant'Elena. This is Venice, remember, so don't be surprised to find an ornate palazzo or treasure-filled church around nearly every corner. START: **Riva degli Schiavoni. Take vaporettos 1, 6, 14, 41, or 42 to the San Zaccaria stop. The church of San Zaccaria is just north along Calle San Zaccaria.**

Clotheslines hang over the canal in Sant'Elena.

1 ★★ **San Zaccaria.** Its location just behind San Marco accounts for the souvenir stands outside and the tombs of several doges inside. This Renaissance/Gothic church dedicated to the father of John the Baptist actually looks like an elaborate picture gallery—the walls are plastered with works by Tiepolo, Tintoretto, Van Dyck, Bellini, and other masters. ⏱ *30 min. Campo San Zaccaria.* ☎ *041-5221257. Mon–Sat 10am–noon, 4–6pm; Sun 4–6pm. Vaporetto: San Zaccaria.*

2 ★ **San Giovanni in Bràgora.** Composer Antonio Vivaldi was baptized here in 1678; the register marking the event is prominently on display. Take time to admire the church's paintings, especially the *Baptism of Christ* by Cima da

Conegliano, behind the altar; the detailed backdrop of rolling hills was inspired by the artist's namesake birthplace north of Venice. ⏱ *15 min. Campo Bandiera e Moro.* ☎ *041-2702464. Mon–Sat 3:30–5:30pm. Vaporetto: Arsenale.*

3 ★★★ **Scuola di San Giorgio degli Schiavoni.** Schiavoni, or Slavs from Dalmatia, prospered in Venice and by the 15th century had acquired the riches to build this scuola (guild house or fraternity) and commission Vittore Carpaccio to paint a sumptuous *Cycle of Saint George*. The master's luminous and detailed depictions of decomposing bodies, ferocious dragons, and out-of-body experiences are captivating. ⏱ *30 min. Calle dei Furlani.* ☎ *041-2750642. 3€. Apr–Oct Tues–Sat 9:30am–12:30pm, 3:30–6:30pm, Sun 9:30am–12:30pm; Nov–Mar Tues–Sat 10am–12:30pm, 3–6pm, Sun 10am–12:30pm. Vaporetto: San Zaccaria.*

4 ★ **Museo della Fondazione Querini Stampalia.** This Renaissance palazzo with modern embellishments houses a small but stunning collection of works by such masters as Pietro Longhi and Giovanni Bellini. The library is a haven for night owls, who are allowed to linger until midnight. ⏱ *45 min. Campo Santa Maria Formosa.* ☎ *041-2711411. Museum: 6€. Library: Free admission. Museum: Tues–Thurs & Sun 10am–10pm; Fri–Sat 10am–10pm. Library: Mon–Fri*

4pm–midnight; Sat 2:30pm–midnight; Sun 3–7pm. *Vaporetto: Rialto.*

5 ★ Chiesa di Santa Maria Formosa. Formosa means "buxom," and this charming 15th-century church honors the image of the Virgin as the fulsome mother of Christ. Fittingly, near the altar is one of the few Venetian masterpieces by a woman, *Allegory of the Foundation of the Church,* an 18th-century work by Guilia Lama. A grotesquely contorted face (one of many startling details you'll encounter in Venice) overlooks the square from the campanile. ⏱ *15 min. Campo Santa Maria Formosa. 2€.* ☎ *041-2750642. Mon–Sat 10am–5pm; Sun 1–5pm. Vaporetto: Rialto.*

6 ★★★ Campo Santi Giovanni e Paolo (San Zanipòlo). Pride of place belongs to Bartolomeo Colleoni, a 15th-century mercenary who requested that a statue be erected in his honor in front of San Marco. The doges obliged with an impressive equestrian monument by Verrocchio, but they deceived the old soldier for all eternity—behind him is the Scuola Grande di San Marco, not the San Marco he had in mind. ⏱ *15 min.*

7 Rosa Salva. Linger over a pastry and cappuccino at this venerable old cafe while admiring the square. *Campo Santi Giovanni e Paolo.* ☎ *041-5227949.*

8 ★★ Basilica di Santi Giovanni e Paolo. One of the largest churches in Venice holds the last remains of numerous doges, whose marble tombs line the lofty nave in a show of dusty pomp. The church's great treasures include ceiling paintings by Giovanni Piazzetta in the Chapel of St. Dominic and those by Paolo Veronese in the Rosary Chapel. ⏱ *30 min. Campo Santi*

The Basilica di Santi Giovanni e Paolo.

Giovanni e Paolo. ☎ *041-5235913. Free admission. Mon–Sat 8am–12:30pm, 3:30–7pm; Sun 3–6pm. Vaporetto: Fondamente Nuove.*

9 ★ Fondamenta Nuove. After your slog through dim churches and picture galleries, you'll welcome the chance to take in some sea air on this long quay-side promenade, the departure point for boats to the outlying islands. Across the water is a vision of trees and marble: San Michele, the cemetery of Venice. For a boat trip to the cemetery island, see p 47, bullet **3**. ⏱ *15 min. Vaporetto: Fondamenta Nuove.*

10 Algiubagiò. Take a seat on the terrace and enjoy a pizza or panino as boats come and go. *Fondamenta Nuove.* ☎ *041-5236084.*

11 ★ San Francesco della Vigna. Once surrounded by vineyards *(vigna),* this stately edifice now rises above a workaday neighborhood of quiet alleyways and smelly canals. The 15th-century facade is by Andrea Palladio (see p 29); Pietro Lombardo sculptures and paintings by Veronese, Giovanni

Bellini, and Antonio de Negroponte grace the simple interior. To clear your head of these depictions of saints and sinners, spend a few minutes in the cloisters. 🕐 *30 min. Campo San Francesco della Vigna.* ☎ *041-5206102. Mon–Sat 8am–12:30pm, 3–6:30pm; Sun 3–6:30pm. Vaporetto: Celestia.*

⓬ ★ Arsenale. Experience the glory days of the shipyards that once equipped the republic's navy, first by admiring the elaborate marble land entrance, modeled after a Roman arch and flanked by lions. Then, stand on the bridge across the water entrance for a look at the Corderia (rope factory). These and other vast structures at one time employed some 16,000 shipbuilders who, in production-line style, could assemble a galley in a few hours. 🕐 *15 min. Campo dell'Arsenale. Vaporetto: Arsenale.*

⓭ ★ Museo Storico Navale. Here are elaborate centuries-old models of Venetian ships and doges' barges, crafted by shipbuilders to show off their final designs. Full-scale craft on display include art collector Peggy Guggenheim's private gondola. 🕐 *1 hr. Campo San Biago.* ☎ *041-5200276. 1.55€. Mon–Fri 8:45am–1:30pm; Sat 8:45am–1pm. Vaporetto: Arsenale.*

⓮ Via Garibaldi. Head inland again past shops and outdoor cafes on this broad avenue (a real rarity in

The Arsenale at night.

Venice), named for the hero of Italian unification. You'll encounter scenes more typical of the working city as you continue on to the Fondamenta Sant'Ana, where, on weekday mornings and evenings, a boisterous floating market supplies the neighborhood with local produce. Look for mounds of purple artichokes *(carciofi)* from the island of Sant'Erasmo and radicchio from the fertile Treviso farmlands. 🕐 *15 min. Vaporetto: Arsenale.*

⓯ ★ San Pietro in Castello. Some of the earliest Venetians settled here (their fortification, Castello, gave the neighborhood its name). The neglected-looking basilica was the official cathedral of Venice until 1807, when the privilege was transferred to San Marco. Inside are second-century mosaics on the front of the altar in the Lando Chapel. In the last week of June, the waterside lawns beneath the leaning campanile are filled with revelers celebrating the Feast of San Pietro. 🕐 *45 min. Campo San Pietro.* ☎ *041-2750642. 2€. Mon–Sat 10am–5pm; Sun 1–5pm. Vaporetto: San Pietro.*

⓰ ★ Biennale and Giardini Publicci. Crowds descend upon the pavilions in these leafy precincts once a year to attend Venice's acclaimed Biennale, an exhibition of contemporary art in odd years and architecture in even years (see p 123). At other times, only birdsong intrudes on the tranquillity, so find a bench and enjoy stunning views over the lagoon. 🕐 *15 min. Vaporetto: Giardini Esposizione.*

⓱ ★ Sant'Elena. Monuments and fine art are not what draws you to the quietest precinct of Venice. Instead, wander the narrow streets for glimpses of everyday life, and discover that in Venice, what passes for ordinary is pretty extraordinary. 🕐 *1 hr. Vaporetto: Sant'Elena.*

Santa Croce & Dorsoduro

0 ——— 1/8 Mi
0 ——— 200 meters

Giardino
Papadopoli

DORSODURO

S. Nicolò
Mendicoli
S. Teresa

Pal.
Condulmèr

Ángelo
Raffaele

Pal.
Ariani
Fondam
Briati

Pal. Bria
Fondam. Rosa

Calle Nuova

Fond. del Rio Nuovo

Casa Tórres

Pal. Suriàn

Pal. Gabrieli-
Dolfin

Pal.
Arnaldi

S. Nicolò
da Tolentino
Istit. Univ. di
Architettura

Palazzo
Marcello

**SANTA
CROCE**

Coll.
Armeno

Palazzo
Zenobia

Inst. Sup.
d'Arte
Applicata
Carmini

Pal.
Foscarini
Fond. Foscarini

Campo
S. Margherita

S. Pantalòn

Stazione
Marittima

Salizz. S. Basegio

S. Sebastiano

Calle Lunga S. Barnaba

Pal. Cornèr
d. Frescada

S. Basilio

Ospedale
G. B. Giustiniàn

Ex Convento
delle Eremite

Pal.
Molin

Pal.
Giustiniàn
Fondam. di Borgo

S. Barnaba

Pal. Giustiniàn
Pal.
Nani

Pal.
Clary

Palazzo
Brandolin

Pal. Loredàn

Pal. Stern

Ca'
Rezzonico

Ca'
Fóscari

Pal. Civràn-
Grimani

Pal.
Balbi

Pálazzo
Moró-Lin
Pal. Grassi

S. Tomà

Campo
S. Trovaso

Pal. Giustiniàn-
Recanati
Accadémia
Gallerie
dell'Accademia

Pal.
Moro

Ca' del
Duca

Palazzo
Mocenigo

**SAN
MARCO**

S. Maria
di Visitaz.
Záttere

Ex
Convento

Gesuati

Pal. Contarini
degli Scrigni

Pal. Falièr

Pal. Giustiniàn-
Lolin

Ponte
dell'Accadémia

Pal. Loredàn

Campo
S. Stefano
S. Stefano

S. Agnese

Pal. Pal. Bárbaro
Contarini
dal Zaffo

Pal.
Loredàn

Pal. da Mula

Palazzo
Pisani

Palazzo
Contarini-
Fasan

Palazzo
Tiépolo

Casa
Stecchini
Palazzo
Cornèr della
Ca' Granda

S. Maurizio
Campo
S. Maurizio

S. Maria
d. Giglio

Rio terrà A. Foscarini
Fondam. Bragadin

Pal. Veniér dei Leóni
(Guggenheim)

Ex Ospedale
degli
Incurabili

Pal. Dário

Ex Convento
Spirito
Santo

Fondamenta Zátrere ai Saloni

Saloni ex
Magazzini
del Sale

Ex Ospizio

S. Maria
d. Giglio

Pal.
Gritti
Pal. Ferro Fini
Palazzo
Genovese

Salute

S. Maria
d. Salute

Dogana
da Mar

Punta della
Dogana

These neighborhoods surround some of the city's greatest treasure houses, including Carmini, the Galleria dell'Accademia, and the Peggy Guggenheim Collection—all reason enough for a visit, of course. But you'll also be enchanted by the area's pleasant squares and little alleyways. START: **Piazzale Roma. Take vaporettos 1, 41, 42, 51, 52, 61, 62, or 82 to the Piazzale Roma stop. Follow the Fondamenta Santa Chiara east to Giardini Papadopoli.**

① ★ Giardino Papadopoli. Many Venetians only know this garden atop the remains of a convent as a quick route to Piazzale Roma. You might want to linger a bit, though, especially on the Esplanade at the edge of the Grand Canal—it's one of the few public spaces on the banks of this scenic waterway. ⏱ *15 min. Vaporetto: Piazzale Roma.*

② ★ San Nicolò da Tolentino. Immerse yourself in the baroque— behind the unfinished facade and portico are frescoes and paintings awash in a swirl of *putti* (pink-cheeked cherubs) and saints, including an ecstatic Saint Francis. Frescoes in the third chapel provide a vivid and gory lesson in the lives of Saint Celia and other saints. ⏱ *20 min. Campo dei Tolentini.* ☎ *041-710806. 2€. Mon–Sat 9:30am–noon, 4–6pm; Sun 4–6pm. Vaporetto: Piazzale Roma.*

③ ★★ San Pantalon. More than 60 ceiling paintings by Gian Antonio Fumiani illustrate *The Martyrdom and Glory of Saint Pantaleon,* the court physician to the Emperor Galerius who was beheaded under Diocletian. Fumiani's story is no less fervent than the saint's—the artist lay on his back for 24 years to execute these dark-hued masterpieces, then fell from a scaffold to his death as he applied the last brush strokes. The church's other treasure is a nail said to be from the true cross, enshrined in a lavish altar. ⏱ *20 min. Campo San Pantalon.* ☎ *041-5235893. 2€. Mon–Sat 4–6pm. Vaporetto: San Tomà.*

④ ★★ Campo Santa Margherita. One of the most appealing squares in Venice is a stage set for market stalls, shops, cafes, and the comings and goings of the neighborhood.

⑤ Gelateria il Doge. Many Venetians argue that Doge serves the best gelato in town. Why not try a scoop or two and see if you agree? *Campo Santa Margherita.* ☎ *041-5234607.*

⑥ ★★★ Scuola dei Carmini. In this perfectly preserved 17th-century bastion of the Carmelite order, the artist Tiepolo steals the show with magnificent ceiling paintings. *See p 32, bullet ⑧.*

⑦ ★ Rio San Barnaba. Follow this canal past lovely houses and a floating market to the Punti dei Pugni (Bridge of the Punches), so-called because rival neighborhood factions were allowed to brawl publicly on the span until the practice

Campo Santa Margherita: street scene.

was banned around 1700. Just beyond, the canal laps against one side of Campo Santa Barnaba, shaded by its namesake church. ⏱ *15 min. Vaporetto: San Basilio.*

⑧ ★ Calle Lunga San Barnaba. Among the many enticing antiques and crafts for sale along this shopping street and surrounding alleys are miniature towns and palaces carved in wood at Signor Blum (www.signorblum.com), Campo San Barnaba. ☎ 041-5226367. ⏱ *15 min. Vaporetto: San Basilio.*

⑨ ★★ San Sebastiano. The artist Paolo Veronese left his mark on this 16th-century church, where he spent most of his career painting a luridly colorful fresco cycle and huge canvases. Queen Esther is opulently clad and bejeweled, and Sebastian is theatrically pierced with arrows. The artist is buried here amid his creations. ⏱ *20 min. See p 32, bullet ⑦.*

⑩ ★ Angelo Raffaele. A gripping story unfolds in the organ loft, where Antonio Guardi's sumptuous paintings relate the archangel's adventure-filled travels, in human form, with Tobias, an early Christian. The elaborately carved well behind

Veronese's Martyrdom of St. Sebastian, in the San Sebastiano church.

the church in Campo Sant'Angelo was the gift of a plague-stricken, 14th-century merchant who mistakenly believed that contaminated water was the cause of his demise and wished to spare others his fate. ⏱ *15 min.* ☎ *041-5228548. 2€. Campo Angelo dell'Raffaele. Mon–Sat 8am–noon, 3–6pm; Sun 3–6:30pm. Vaporetto: San Basilio.*

⑪ ★ San Nicolò Mendicoli. "Mendicoli" are beggars, and the poor once took shelter under the portico of this church. The second-oldest church in Venice (after San Giacomo di Rialto) dates from the 7th century. Rebuilt in the 12th century, it has a massive bell tower and other telltale Byzantine features. Of more recent note, the church appeared in the engagingly creepy 1973 cult film *Don't Look Now.* ⏱ *20 min. San Nicolò Mendicoli.* ☎ *041-2750382. Mon–Sat 10am–noon. Vaporetto: San Basilio.*

⑫ ★ Zattere. This busy quay is named for the rafts that arrived here during the days of the Republic laden with wood to build ships and palaces. Across the canal, a deep-water channel that is often choked with boat traffic, is the island of Giudecca (see p 46); Il Redentore, the impressive dome-topped church designed by Palladio; and other imposing structures that line the island's waterfront. ⏱ *15 min. Vaporetto: Zattere.*

⑬ ★ Squero San Trovaso. This shipyard builds and repairs gondolas—a uniquely Venetian operation. The yard's wooden buildings, bedecked with balconies and window boxes, are quite picturesque. A stroll along Fondamenta Nani (fondamenta is a street or quay along a canal) affords an excellent view of the goings-on. ⏱ *15 min. Vaporetto: Zattere.*

⑭ ★ San Trovaso. Dedicated to two saints, Gervasius and Protasius,

People strolling along the Zattere.

this elegant 17th-century church has two similar facades, one at each end, an arrangement allegedly made so that the members of the two warring factions who worshipped here could enter and leave the church without bloodshed. Inside are paintings by two Tintorettos: a *Temptation of Saint Anthony* and *Last Supper* by Jacopo, known as Il Tintoretto, and three canvases by his son Dominic. ⏱ *20 min. Campo San Trovaso.* ☎ *041-2702464. Mon–Sat 3–6pm. Vaporetto: Zattere.*

⑮ ★ Santa Maria del Rosario ai Gesuati. When the Dominican order took over this waterfront church in the 18th century, they commissioned paintings and frescoes of Saint Dominic and other saints. Giambattista Tiepolo had the honor of depicting Dominic's life in a series

of colorful ceiling panels. ⏱ *20 min. Fondamenta Zattere ai Gesuati.* ☎ *041-2750642. 2€. Mon–Sat 10am–5pm; Sun 1–5pm. Vaporetto: Zattere.*

⑯ ★ Rio Terrá Foscarini. This shop-lined street leads north from the Zattere to the Grand Canal and the Accademia Bridge. Wander off the Rio into some of the adjoining alleys to get a sense of the quiet neighborhood. ⏱ *15 min. Vaporetto: Zattere or Accademia.*

⑰ ★★★ Gallerie dell'Accademia. Viewing Carpaccio's *Ursula* cycle in room 21 and Gentile Bellini's *Procession in St. Mark's Square* cycle is like gazing up at the Milky Way: Another splendid detail emerges with every blink of the eye. *See p 34.*

⑱ ★★★ Museum Café at the Peggy Guggenheim Collection. Enjoy a coffee or glass of wine on the cafe terrace overlooking the garden and the Grand Canal. ⏱ *30 min. See p 11, bullet ④.*

⑲ ★★ Salute and Dogana da Mar. The prospect of seeing the Grand Canal, San Marco, and the lagoon from this remarkable church and Customs house supplies a dramatic ending to your walk. *See p 11, bullet ①.*

A gondola being raised in the the the Squero San Trovaso shipyard.

Cannaregio & the Ghetto

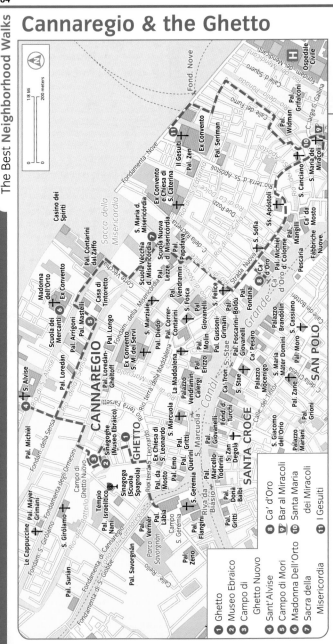

0   1/8 Mi
0   200 meters

1 Ghetto
2 Museo Ebraico
3 Campo di Ghetto Nuovo
4 Sant'Alvise
5 Campo di Mori
6 Madonna Dell'Orto
7 Sacra della Misericordia
8 Ca' d'Oro
9 Bar al Miracoli
10 Santa Maria dei Miracoli
11 I Gesuiti

Venice gets down to everyday business in this sprawling neighborhood, which stretches north from the Grand Canal to the lagoon—the train station is here, as are many shops. You'll discover quiet squares and one splendid art-filled church after another. START: Campo Ghetto Nuevo. Take vaporettos 41, 42, 51, or 52 to the Ponte Guglie stop. From there, the Sottoportego di Ghetto Vecchio leads northeast through the Campo delle Scuole to the Campo di Ghetto Nuovo.

The Casa Israelitica di Riposo synagogue in the Ghetto.

❶ ★ Ghetto. The term "geto" originated in Venice and referred to a medieval foundry where metals for cannons were cast. Until Napoleon conquered Venice in 1797, Jews were allowed to live only in the Ghetto. Even though only a few kosher restaurants and food shops remain, the neighborhood still feels cut off from the rest of the city. 🕐 *15 min. Vaporetto: Ponte de Guglie.*

❷ ★ Museo Ebraico. The most memorable part of a visit to this small museum celebrating Venetian Judaism is the guided tour of three synagogues that occupy the top floors of nearby houses and are easily recognized from the street by their five distinctive windows. 🕐 *1 hr. Campo Ghetto Nuevo.* 📞 *041-715359. www.museoebraico.it. 3€ museum, 8€ museum and synagogue tour. Oct–May Sun–Fri 10am–4pm; June–Sept Sun–Fri 10–7pm. Vaporetto: Ponte de Guglie.*

❸ ★★ Campo di Ghetto Nuovo. The extraordinary height of the houses around this square testifies to the overcrowded conditions in the Ghetto; prevented from expanding into other parts of the city, residents could only build up. A monument of bas-relief panels commemorates Venetian Jews deported by the Nazis. 🕐 *15 min. Vaporetto: Ponte de Guglie.*

❹ ★ Sant'Alvise. Lurid canvases of the *Flagellation* and the *Road to Calvary* by Gianbattista Tiepolo are the masterpieces here, but they are not as enchanting as the eight, almost primitive tempura paintings of biblical scenes by an unknown 15th-century artist from the school of Lazzaro Bastiani. 🕐 *30 min. Campo Sant'Alvise.* 📞 *041-2750462. 2€. Mon–Sat 10am–5pm; Sun 1–5pm. Vaporetto: Sant'Alvise.*

❺ ★ Campo di Mori. Three 13th-century statues are the de facto guardians of this quiet square. The figures are allegedly three Moorish brothers who made their fortunes trading with the Near East and built a palazzo nearby. Tintoretto, the greatest of the Venetian masters, lived in a canal-side house just around the corner from the square on Fondamenta dei Mori until his death in 1594. 🕐 *15 min. Vaporetto: Madonna dell'Orto.*

❻ ★★ Madonna Dell'Orto. Tintoretto is buried in his neighborhood church, surrounded by several of his works. Tintoretto commemorates the martyrdom of Saint Christopher in his *Beheading of Saint Christopher.*

🕐 *30 min. Campo Madonna Dell'Orto.* ☎ *041-2750642. 2 €. Mon–Sat 10am–5pm; Sun 1–5pm. Vaporetto: Madonna dell'Orto.*

7 ★ **Sacra della Misericordia.** The end of the canal-side Fondamenta di Gasparo Contarini provides a perfect perch from which to take in the view over the Sacra, a protected cove in the lagoon where all manner of colorful craft can be seen. 🕐 *15 min. Vaporetto: Madonna dell'Orto.*

8 ★★★ **Ca' d'Oro.** An alley leads off busy Strada Nuova, an atypically straight avenue laid out in the 1860s to facilitate foot traffic to and from the railway station, to a far more pleasing setting—this ornate Gothic palazzo on the banks of the Grand Canal. If you haven't seen the masterpieces in the palazzo's Galleria Franchetti, step inside. *See p 39, bullet* **8**.

9 🍵 **Bar al Miracoli.** Panini and other snacks are served at outdoor tables in a pretty campo. *Campo Santa Maria Nova.* ☎ *041-5231515.*

10 ★★★ **Santa Maria dei Miracoli.** A top contender for the most beautiful church in Venice is sheathed in gleaming white marble; the effect is especially stunning when the exterior is lit at night. Inside, painted panels in the barrel-vaulted ceiling depict the prophets.

The church of Santa Maria dei Miracoli.

🕐 *30 min. Campo Santa Maria dei Miracoli.* ☎ *041-2750462. 2 €. Mon–Sat 10am–5pm; Sun 1–5pm. Vaporetto: Rialto.*

11 ★ **I Gesuiti.** The Venetian outpost of the Jesuit order is tucked away in a quiet neighborhood of narrow alleys and simple houses. These humble surroundings belie the extravagant baroque fantasy inside—the apse and side chapels are festooned with tromp l'oeil drapery swags, unfurling carpets, and brocaded ropes, all fashioned from green and white marble. 🕐 *20 min. Campo dei Gesuiti.* ☎ *041-5286579. Daily 10am–noon, 4–6pm. Vaporetto: Fondamenta Nuove.* ●

The Jews of Venice

Jews began settling in Venice in great numbers in the 16th century, and the republic soon came to value their services as moneylenders, physicians, and traders. For centuries the Jewish population was forced to live on an island that now encompasses the Campo Ghetto Nuovo, and drawbridges were raised to enforce a nighttime curfew. By the end of the 17th century, as many as 5,000 Jews lived in the Ghetto's cramped confines. Today, the city's Jewish population is comprised of about 500 people, few of whom live in the Ghetto.

Shopping **Best Bets**

Best Recordings of Baroque Music
★★ Vivaldi Store, *Salizzada del Fontego dei Tedeschi, San Marco* (p 74)

Best Way to See All of Venice at a Glance
★★★ Il Mondo in Miniatura, *Calle della Toletta, Dorsoduro* (p 76)

Best Place to Dip Your Oar in the Water
★★★ Spazio Legno, *Fondamenta San Giacomo, Giudecca* (p 76)

Best Way to Stock Up on Pasta You'll Never Put in a Pot of Boiling Water
★★ Giacomo Rizzo, *Calle San Giovanni Crisostomo, Cannaregio* (p 78)

Best Goblets with a Pedigree
★★★ Barovier and Tasso, *Fondamenta dei Vetrai 28, Murano* (p 78)

Best Views of the Grand Canal from a Shop
★★★ Genninger Studio, *Calle del Traghetto, Dorsoduro* (p 79)

Best Gifts for the Folks Back Home
★★ Gugliemo Sent, *Fondamenta Vetrai, Murano* (p 79)

Best Place to String a Necklace
★★ Perle e Dintorni, *Calle della Mandola, San Marco* (p 81)

Best Chance to Shod Yourself in Stylish Comfort
★★★ Fratelli Rossetti, *Salizzada San Moisé, San Marco* (p 81)

Best Sources for Exquisite Lace Doilies
★★★ Jeserum, *Piazza San Marco, San Marco* (p 82); and ★★★ Martinuzzi, *Piazza San Marco, San Marco* (p 82)

Best Place to Hide Behind a Mask
★★★ MondoNovo, *Rio Terrà Canal, Dorsoduro* (p 83)

Best Stationery that's Sure to Impress
★★★ Legatoria Piazzesi, *Campiello Feltrina, San Marco* (p 84)

Best Place to Pretend to be a Gondolier
★★★ Gilberto Penzo, *Calle Saoneri, San Polo.* (p 75)

Best Gloves in Town
★★★ Marforio, *Campo San Salvador, San Marco* (p 77)

Best Silk Ties that Look Like Paper
★★ Ebru di Federica Novello, *Campo San Stefano, San Marco* (p 84)

Best Place to Come Face to Face with an Adriatic Sea Creature
★★★ Pescaria Market, *between Campo delle Beccarie and the Canal Grande* (p 82)

Best Paperweights
★★ Sergio Tiozzo, *Fondamenta Manin, Murano* (p 80)

San Marco & Castello **Shopping**

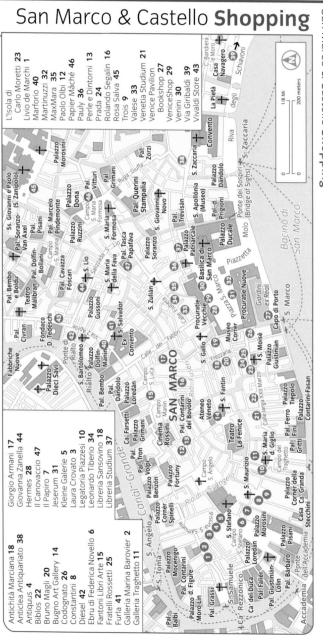

Cannaregio **Shopping**

COIN **4**
Giacomo Rizzo **5**
Lili e Paolo Darin **1**
Mercatino dei
  Miracoli **6**
San Leonardo
  (market) **2**
Standa **3**

Murano **Shopping**

Barovier and Tasso **2**
Berengo **3**
Elite Murano **9**
Gugliemo Sent **4**
La Murrina **1**
Marco Polo **6**
Mazzega **8**
Murano
  Collezioni **7**
Sergio Tiozzo **5**

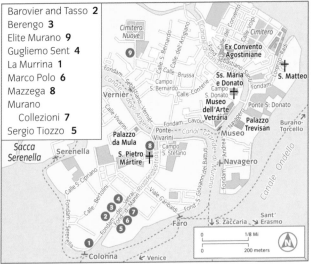

Dorsoduro & Giudecca **Shopping**

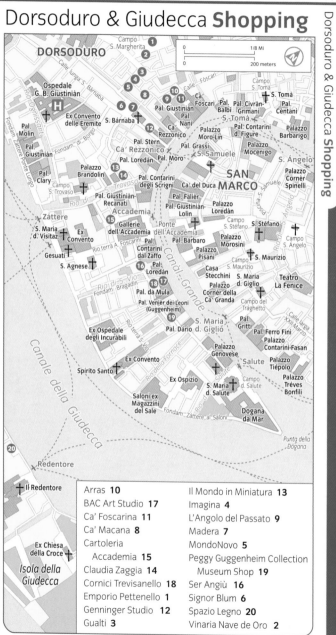

San Polo & Santa Croce **Shopping**

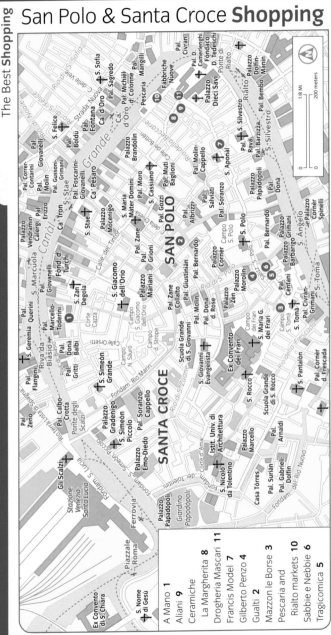

Venice Shopping A to Z

Straw gondolier hats for sale.

Antiques

★★ **Antiquus** SAN MARCO What holds the wide-ranging collection of old paintings, silver, china, and jewelry together is an eye for the highest quality. *Calle delle Botteghe.* ☎ *041-5206395. AE, DC, MC, V. Vaporetto: San Samuele. Map p 69.*

★★ **Kleine Galerie** SAN MARCO This appealingly crowded shop is the best place in town to find an old print of Venice. *Calle delle Botteghe.* ☎ *041-5222177. No credit cards. Vaporetto: Sant'Angelo. Map p 69.*

Art

★ **BAC Art Studio** DORSODURO Prints by local artists are quite affordable, and a wide range of photographic reproductions of Venetian scenes are also available. *Campo San Vio.* ☎ *041-5228171. MC, V. Vaporetto: Accademia. Map p 71.*

★★ **Bugno Art Gallery** SAN MARCO Venetians and other contemporary Italian artists are represented in this large, airy space, where the small, museum-like permanent collection includes works by DeChirico and other Italian greats. *Campo San Fantin.* ☎ *041-5231305. www.bugno artgallery.it. AE, DC, MC, V. Vaporetto: Santa Maria del Giglio. Map p 69.*

★ **Cartoleria Accademia** DORSODURO Has Venice inspired you to pick up a brush? This well-stocked shop has been supplying artists for almost 200 years. *Campiello Calbo.* ☎ *041-5207086. AE, MC, V. Vaporetto: Accademia. Map p 71.*

★★ **Galleria Traghetto** SAN MARCO One of Venice's most

Opening Times

In the old days, Venetian shopkeepers took Sundays and Monday mornings or Wednesday afternoons off, but in these modern times only neighborhood grocers and other local services tend to keep traditional hours. Many Venice shops are now open 7 days a week, especially during the busy summer season and Carnivale. Shopping hours are from around 9am to 1pm and 3 or 4pm to 7:30 or 8pm, though many shops that cater to tourists forgo the long lunch and keep the doors open throughout the day.

respected galleries is well known for showing works by the city's sizable community of painters and sculptors, with an emphasis on abstract painting. *Calle di Piovan.* ☎ *041-5221188. AE, DC, MC, V. Vaporetto: Santa Maria del Giglio. Map p 69.*

★★ **Imagina** DORSODURO A gallery that seems as evocative as its name features photography, and Venice is the inspiration for many of the works. *Rio Terrà Canal.* ☎ *041-2410625. No credit cards. Vaporetto: Ca' Rezzonico. Map p 71.*

Books & Music

★ **Ca' Foscarina** DORSODURO The bookstore of the University of Venice carries the city's largest selection of books in English, on a wide variety of subjects. *Campiello degli Squellini.* ☎ *041-5229602. AE, DC, MC, V. Vaporetto: San Tomà. Map p 71.*

★★ **Fantoni Libri Arte** SAN MARCO Lavishly illustrated volumes on art, photography, and design fill the tables, making this the perfect stop to find a coffee-table book to take home. *Salizzada San Luca.* ☎ *041-5220700. AE, DC, MC, V. Vaporetto: Rialto. Map p 69.*

Floating vegetable market.

★★★ **Libreria Sansovino** SAN MARCO One of Venice's most venerable bookstores carries antiquarian books as well as lavish volumes on Venetian art; the stock also includes a good selection of English-language titles. *Bacino Orseolo.* ☎ *041-5222623. AE, DC, MC, V. Vaporetto: San Marco/Vallaresso. Map p 69.*

★ **Libreria Studium** SAN MARCO A good stop for English-language travel guides, as well as some vacation reading—the selection of fiction and nonfiction from England and the U.S. is fairly extensive. *Calle Canonica.* ☎ *041-5222382. AE, DC, MC, V. Vaporetto: San Zaccaria. Map p 69.*

★★ **Peggy Guggenheim Collection Museum Shop** DORSODURO Among the lavishly illustrated volumes on modern art, photography, and Venice are many fine European editions. *Fondamenta Venier dal Leoni.* ☎ *041-2405424. AE, DC, MC, V. Vaporetto: Accademia. Map p 71.*

★★ **Venice Pavilion Bookshop** SAN MARCO The bookshop of the Venice tourism office is amply stocked with guidebooks and maps, as well as handsome volumes on Venetian art and architecture. *Giardinetti Reali.* ☎ *041-5226356. AE, DC, MC, V. Vaporetto: San Zaccaria. Map p 69.*

★★ **Vivaldi Store** SAN MARCO Works by the eponymous composer and other masters line the shelves. *Salizzada del Fontego dei Tedeschi.* ☎ *041-5221343. MC, V. Vaporetto: Rialto. Map p 69.*

Crafts

★ **A Mano** SANTA CROCE True to the name, everything—mirrors, picture frames, lamps, and other decorative items—is handmade and

Ceramiche La Margherita shop near the Rialto Bridge.

one of a kind. *Rio Terrà.* ☎ 041-715742. MC, V. Vaporetto: San Tomà. Map p 72.

★★ **Antichità Marciana** SAN MARCO   Hand-painted velvets, sold by the meter, make unique coverings for cushions and are works of art in themselves, ideal as wall hangings. *Frezzeria.* ☎ 041-5235666. AE, DC, MC, V. Vaporetto: San Marco/Vallaresso. Map p 69.

★ **Arras** DORSODURO   Woolens and silks are woven by a cooperative that employs the disabled. *Campiello Squellini.* ☎ 041-5226460. AE, DC, MC, V. Map p 71.

★★★ **Ceramiche La Margherita** SANTA CROCE   Margherita Rossetto is a master ceramics craftsperson, producing teapots, cups, and other items that she then hand-paints in charming designs. Prices in her little shop near the Ponte di Rialto are remarkably reasonable. *Sottoportico della Siora Bettina.* ☎ 041-723120.

Venetian character puppet.

www.lamargheritavenezia.com. AE, MC, V. Vaporetto: San Stae. Map p 72.

★★ **Cornici Trevisanello** DORSODURO   This studio specializes in picture frames adorned with gold leaf, ceramic, and glass inlays and other tasteful touches. *Campo San Vio.* ☎ 041-5207779. MC, V. Vaporetto: Accademia. Map p 71.

★★ **Emporio Pettenello** DORSODURO   Puppets, model boats, and other toys, many crafted from wood, are elevated to fine crafts pieces. *Campo Santa Margherita.* ☎ 041-5231167. AE, MC, V. Vaporetto: Ca'Rezzonico. Map p 71.

★★★ **Gilberto Penzo** SAN POLO   If you marveled over the models of doges' craft in the Museo Storico Navale (see p 59, bullet ⑬), you'll be charmed by these wooden replicas of gondolas and other boats. Signori Penzo's replicas may not fit your budget, but you may be able to take home a build-your-own kit. *Calle Saoneri.* ☎ *041-719372. MC, V. Vaporetto: San Tomà. Map p 72.*

★★★ Il Mondo in Miniatura

DORSODURO As if Venice weren't whimsical enough, Giovanni Moro re-creates the city's palaces and other architectural wonders in fanciful miniatures. It's well worth stopping by the shop just to see his scale model of the entire city. *UPDATE: Store now closed permanently.*

★ Livio de Marchi SAN MARCO

There's not a practical item in sight, but this studio's wooden models of socks, chairs, and other everyday items are becoming known around the world. *Salizzada San Samuele.* ☎ *041-5285694. www.liviodemarchi.com. AE, DC, MC, V. Vaporetto: San Samuele. Map p 69.*

★ Madera DORSODURO Wooden

bowls, vases, and other household items are boldly designed, as are the ceramics and other pieces on display. *Campo San Barnaba.* ☎ *041-5224181. www.maderavenezia.com. AE, MC, V. Vaporetto: Ca' Rezzonico. Map p 71.*

★★ Sabbie e Nebbie SAN POLO

The beautiful pottery and ceramics are from Japan and Italy. *Calle dei Nomboli.* ☎ *041-719073. MC, V. Vaporetto: San Tomà. Map p 72.*

★★ Signor Blum DORSODURO

A group of local women fashion wonderful models of Venetian mon-uments as well as fairy-tale castles and palaces. The shop's signature painted wooden panels of Venetian scenes are also alluring. *Campo San Barnaba.* ☎ *041-5211399. www. signorblum.com. MC, V. Vaporetto: Ca' Rezzonico. Map p 71.*

★★★ Spazio Legno GUIDECCA

The serious business at hand here is making oars, oar rests *(forcoli),* and other wooden components for gon-dolas. Visitors can watch work in progress and walk away with one of the wooden bookmarks shaped like a *forcola* and other small objects the shop makes from its remnants. *Fon-damenta San Giacomo.* ☎ *041-2775505. AE, DC, MC, V. Vaporetto: Redentore. Map p 71.*

★★ Trois SAN MARCO Become

inspired by the creations of Spanish designer Mariano Fortuny on display in his home, Palazzo Fortuny (see p 37, bullet ③), then come here to shop for vintage Fortuny fabrics. *Campo San Maurizio.* ☎ *041-5222905. AE, DC, MC, V. Vaporetto: Santa Maria del Giglio. Map p 69.*

★★ Valese SAN MARCO Stop in

to see the art of bronze casting; the output includes small statuary and other decorative items. *Calle Fiu-bera.* ☎ *041-5227282. AE, MC, V. Vaporetto: San Marco/Vallaresso. Map p 69.*

★★ Venetia Studium SAN

MARCO Fortuny-style designs are the distinctive hallmarks of the shops' stunning lamps in silk and glass, and also find their way onto

Fortuny lampshades at Venetia Studium.

everything from scarves to pillows. *Calle Larga XXII.* ☎ *041-5229281. www.venetiastudium.com. AE, DC, MC, V. Vaporetto: Santa Maria del Giglio. Map p 69.*

Department Stores

★ **COIN** CANNAREGIO High fashion, designer housewares, cosmetics, and other appealing items are on offer in this branch of one of Italy's higher-end chain. *San Giovanni Crisostomo.* ☎ *041-520358. AE, DC, MC, V. Vaporetto: Rialto. Map p 70.*

★★ **Standa** CANNAREGIO Sensible, run-of-the-mill clothing and household goods fill the shelves; the supermarket is a gourmand's paradise and a good place to stock up on Italian delicacies. *UPDATE: Store now closed permanently*

Fashion

★★ **Codognato** SAN MARCO One of Italy's better-known jewelers caters to an international clientele. *Calle Seconda dell'Ascensione.* ☎ *041-5225042. AE, DC, MC, V. Vaporetto: San Marco/Vallaresso. Map p 69.*

★★★ **Francis Model** SAN POLO A family business fashions briefcases, bags, and other goods in beautiful leather. *Ruga del Ravano.* ☎ *041-5212889. AE, DC, MC, V. Vaporetto: San Silvestro. Map p 72.*

★★ **Giovanna Zanella** SAN MARCO Giovanni, who's quickly becoming known as one of Italy's more innovative designers, sells her fine line of stylish women's clothing and accessories from this delightful shop. *Campo San Lio.* ☎ *041-5235500. AE, DC, MC, V. Vaporetto: Rialto. Map p 69.*

★★ **Gualti** DORSODURO The distinctive contemporary jewelry is

made on the premises. *Rio Terrà Canal.* ☎ *041-5201731. www.gualti. it. AE, DC, MC, V. Vaporetto: Ca' Rezzonico. Map p 71.*

★★ **Il Grifone** SAN POLO The high-quality leather belts, wallets, and other goods are all handmade. *Fondamenta del Gaffaro.* ☎ *041-5229452. AE, DC, MC, V. Vaporetto: Piazzale Roma.*

★ **Laura Crovato** SAN MARCO A good selection of secondhand women's clothing and jewelry often yields some remarkable buys. *Calle delle Botteghe.* ☎ *041-5204170. MC, V. Vaporetto: Sant' Angelo. Map p 69.*

★★★ **Marforio** SAN MARCO Venice's preferred leather shop since 1875 sells top-of-the-line wallets, gloves, bags, and other accessories. *Campo San Salvador.* ☎ *041-5225734. AE, DC, MC, V. Vaporetto: Rialto. Map p 69.*

★★ **Mazzon le Borse** SAN POLO Any Venetian can lead you to this store, a well-known local favorite for high-quality, handmade leather goods. *Campiello San Tomà.* ☎ *041-5203421. AE, DC, MC, V. Vaporetto: San Tomà. Map p 72.*

★★ **Rolando Segalin** SAN MARCO If a pair of handmade Italian shoes in fine leather is on your wish list, here's the place to fulfill it. *Calle dei Fuseri.* ☎ *041-5222115. AE, DC, MC, V. Vaporetto: Rialto. Map p 69.*

★ **Ser Angiù** DORSODURO Designer labels at discounted prices—a winning formula that draws crowds of local shoppers. *Piscina del Forner.* ☎ *041-5231149. MC, V. Vaporetto: Accademia. Map p 71.*

Food

★ **Aliani** SAN POLO The perfect place to stock up on hotel-room

Sandwiches for sale in takeout food shops.

provisions—wine, cheese, and meats from all over Italy fill the busy, aromatic shop. *Ruga Rialto.* ☎ *041-5224913. No credit cards. Vaporetto: San Silvestro. Map p 72.*

★★★ **Drogheria Mascari** SAN POLO   Step in to savor the aromas of spices, coffees, and teas. Huge jars are filled with dried fruits, nuts, and sweets. The selection of olive oil, vinegar, and wine from throughout Italy is probably the best in the city. *Ruga degli Spezieri.* ☎ *041-5229762. No credit cards. Vaporetto: San Silvestro. Map p 72.*

★★ **Giacomo Rizzo** CANNAREGIO Basic foodstuffs fill the shelves, but the draw is the pasta—in dozens of shapes and colors. Many, such as those shaped like carnival masks, are too beautiful to eat. *Calle San Giovanni Crisostomo.* ☎ *041-5222824. AE, DC, MC, V. Vaporetto: Rialto. Map p 70.*

★★★ **Rosa Salva** CASTELLO One of the city's most renowned pastry shops is a popular place to sit and linger over a sweet treat and a cappuccino, but you can also take home the tempting baked goods. *Campo Santi Giovanni e Paolo.* ☎ *041-5227949. No credit cards. Vaporetto: Fondamenta Nove. Map p 69.*

★ **Vinaria Nave de Oro** DORSO-DURO   Locals bring their own containers for a fill-up from huge vats of regional wines, also available by the bottle. *Campo Santa Margherita.* ☎ *041-5222693. No credit cards. Vaporetto: Ca' Rezzonico. Map p 71.*

Glass

★★★ **Barovier and Tasso** MURANO   The most prestigious glass shop in Venice traces its roots to the 13th century. With a lineage like that, and with such creations to its credit as the Bouvier Wedding Cup, a Renaissance masterpiece, the shop's creations are regarded as museum pieces by all but a fortunate few. *Fondamenta dei Vetrai 28.* ☎ *041-5274385. www.barovier.com. AE, DC, MC, V. Vaporetto: Colonna. Map p 70.*

★★★ **Berengo** MURANO   One of Murano's best-known glassworks specializes in glass sculpture and platters, vases, and other items that are more decorative than functional. *Fondamenta dei Vetrai 109.* ☎ *041-5276364. www.berengo.com. AE, DC, MC, V. Vaporetto: Colonna. Map p 70.*

★★ **Elite Murano** MURANO   The house specializes in exquisite and often colorful reproductions of traditional Venetian goblets and other glassware. *Calle del Cimitero 6.*

041-736168. AE, MC, V. Vaporetto: Venier. Map p 70.

★★ Galleria Marina Barovier

SAN MARCO One of the city's top showplaces for contemporary designers, run by a member of a distinguished line of glass crafters, also specializes in classic 20th-century pieces by Venetian artisans. *Salizzada San Samuele.* ☎ *041-5226102. www.barovier.it. No credit cards. Vaporetto: San Samuele. Map p 69.*

★★★ Genninger Studio DORSO-

DURO A paneled salon overlooking the Grand Canal is a showcase for Byzantine-style oil lamps, goblets, jewelry embellished with silver and gold, and other glass creations by Leslie Ann Genninger. *Calle del Traghettoo.* ☎ *041-5225565. www. genningerstudio.com. AE, DC, MC, V. Vaporetto: Ca' Rezzonico. Map p 71.*

★★ Gugliemo Sent MURANO

One of Murano's longer-established glass houses has a fine array of paperweights, picture frames, and other tasteful gifts. *Fondamenta Vetrai.* ☎ *041-739100. AE, DC, MC, V. Vaporetto: Colonna. Map p 70.*

★★ La Murrina MURANO The

modern glass pieces are among some of the finest produced on Murano. *Piazzale Colonna.* ☎ *041-5274605. AE, DC, MC, V. Vaporetto: Colonna. Map p 70.*

Vintage Venetian vases and glasses, pictured here in a salted paper print from 1855.

★★ L'Angolo del Passato DOR-

SODURO The superb collections of vintage glass include 19th- and 20th-century Murano pieces rarely on offer; contemporary artisans are represented as well. *Calle del Capeller.* ☎ *041-5287896. AE, DC, MC, V. Vaporetto: Ca' Rezzonico. Map p 71.*

★★ Leonardo Tiberio SAN

MARCO Many of the sophisticated designs are family creations, and works by other local artisans are

Detail from glass in the Berengo collection, on the island of Murano.

Store window of the famed Venini glass shop.

represented, alongside vintage pieces. *Calle Fubiero.* ☎ *041-5232250. AE, DC, MC, V. Vaporetto: San Marco/Vallaresso. Map p 69.*

★★ **L'Isola di Carlo Moretti** SAN MARCO   One of Venice's top glass designers is known internationally for his colorful, often functional wares, making his shop especially alluring. *Campo San Moisè.* ☎ *041-5231973. AE, DC, MC, V. Vaporetto: San Marco/Vallaresso. Map p 69.*

★ **Marco Polo** MURANO   Watch glassblowers at work in the studio of this large concern, where the output ranges from attractive, everyday glassware to museum-quality pieces. *Fondamenta Manin 1.* ☎ *041-739904. AE, DC, MC, V. Vaporetto: Colonna. Map p 70.*

★ **Mazzega** MURANO   Chandeliers and glass sculptures are specialties of the house. Visitors are invited in to see pieces being made. *Fondamenta da Mula.* ☎ *041-736888. www.mazzega.it. AE, DC, MC, V. Vaporetto: Venier. Map p 70.*

★★ **Murano Collezioni** MURANO   A one-stop shop selling the creations of some of Murano's better glassmakers. *Fondamenta Manin.* ☎ *041-736272. AE, DC, MC, V. Vaporetto: Colonna. Map p 70.*

★ **Pauly** SAN MARCO   The output of several Murano glass factories is sold here at prices that aren't discounted but are quite reasonable, especially given the prestigious San Marco location. *Calle Larga San Marco.* ☎ *041-5209899. www.pauly glassfactory.com. AE, DC, MC, V. Vaporetto: San Marco/Vallaresso. Map p 69.*

★★ **Sergio Tiozzo** MURANO   The specialty of the house is *murrine,* a technique in which glass flowers are melted together to form colorful mosaic patterns. The designs are well suited to decorative pieces, not to mention plates, glassware, and vases. *Fondamenta Manin.* ☎ *041-5274155. AE, MC, V. Vaporetto: Faro. Map p 70.*

★ **VeniceShop** SAN MARCO   It's difficult to walk out without an upscale souvenir in hand, be it a glass ornament or a set of glasses; prices are extremely reasonable. *Piazza San Marco.* ☎ *041-5285899. AE, DC, MC, V. Vaporetto: San Marco/Vallaresso. Map p 69.*

★★ **Venini** SAN MARCO   The standard-bearer of all Venetian glass shops, a fixture on the Piazza San Marco since the 1920s, has been bought by a foreign corporation, but remains an essential stop. Top designers from around the world still create exquisite contemporary designs for the shop. *Piazza San Marco.* ☎ *041-5224045.*

www.venini.com. AE, DC, MC, V.
Vaporetto: San Marco/Vallaresso.
Map p 69.

Glass Beads

★ **Anticlea Antiquariato**
CASTELLO   Many of the beads here
are antique and rare treasures; the
new creations are also exquisite.
Campo San Provolo. ☎ 041-5286946.
AE, DC, MC, V. Vaporetto: San Zaccaria. Map p 69.

★ **Claudia Zaggia** DORSODURO
Glass beads are made into jewelry,
ornaments, and other decorative
items. Calle de la Toletta. ☎ 041-
5223159. AE, MC, V. Vaporetto:
Accademia. Map p 71.

★ **Constantini** SAN MARCO
Ready-made bracelets as well as
hundreds of variations of colorful
beads are very well priced. Campo
San Maurizio. [tel[041-5210789. MC,
V. Vaporetto: Santa Maria del Giglio.
Map p 69.

★★ **Lili e Paolo Darin** CANNARE-
GIO   Beads in this enticing shop
are one-of-a-kind creations, strung
together into beautiful and affordable bracelets and necklaces.
Salizada Santa Geremia. ☎ 041-
7175770. MC, V. Vaporetto: San Marcuola. Map p 70.

★★ **Perle e Dintorni** SAN
MARCO   The exotic beads here
recall Venice at the height of its maritime powers—based on age-old
designs, they show Byzantine,
Asian, and African influences. Buy
them by the piece and the shop will
help you string together a bracelet
or necklace. Calle della Mandola.
☎ 041-5205068. AE, DC, MC, V.
Vaporetto: Sant'Angelo. Map p 69.

Italian/European Designers
★ **Bruno Magli** SAN MARCO
Luxurious, beautifully made shoes
that last a lifetime are on offer here

and at several other outlets around
the San Marco neighborhood.
Frezzeria. ☎ 041-5223472. AE,
DC, MC, V. Vaporetto: San Marco/
laresso. Map p 69.

★ **Diesel** SAN MARCO   The hip
firm that's made a fortune clothing
fashionable youth in extravagantly
priced jeans is based here in the
Veneto. Salizada Pio X. ☎ 041-
2411937. AE, DC, MC, V. Vaporetto:
Rialto. Map p 69.

★★★ **Fratelli Rossetti** SAN
MARCO   This family-run concern is
dedicated to making what must be
some of the world's most comfortable shoes. Salizzada San Moisé.
☎ 041-5220819. AE, DC, MC, V.
Vaporetto: San Marco/Vallaresso.
Map p 69.

★ **Furla** SAN MARCO   This international chain can't be beat for stylish,
well-made leather bags. Marzaria San
Salvador. ☎ 041-2770460. AE, DC,
MC, V. Vaporetto: Rialto. Map p 69.

★ **Giorgio Armani** SAN MARCO
Fashions for men and women are
classics that never go out of style.
Calle Carlo Goldoni. ☎ 041-5234758.
AE, DC, MC, V. Vaporetto: San Zac-
caria. Map p 69.

★ **Hermès** SAN MARCO   The
French purveyor of leather bags
and silk scarves occupies one of the
choicest addresses in town. Piazza
San Marco. ☎ 041-5210117. AE, DC,
MC, V. Vaporetto: San Zaccaria. Map
p 69.

★ **MaxMara** SAN MARCO
Another family-run concern, based
in nearby Parma, MaxMara never
misses the mark with stylish frocks
and accessories. Marzaria del'Orlo-
gio. ☎ 041-5226688. AE, DC, MC, V.
Vaporetto: San Zaccaria. Map p 69.

★ **Prada** SAN MARCO   No extravagant shopping spree, or truly stylish wardrobe, would be complete

A lovely example of Burano lacework.

without a little something from this chic designer. *Salizzada San Moisè.* ☎ *041-5283966. AE, DC, MC, V. Vaporetto: San Marco/Vallaresso. Map p 69.*

Lace
★★★ **Jeserum** SAN MARCO
Venice's most renowned purveyor of lace traces its origins to Burano almost 150 years ago and still produces exquisitely embroidered linens and towels. Don't let the prices put you off: Affordable items on offer include linen coasters and napkins. *Piazza San Marco.*

☎ *041-5229864. www.jeserum.it. AE, DC, MC, V. Vaporetto: San Marco/Vallaresso. Map p 69.*

★★★ **Martinuzzi** SAN MARCO
The neighbor and only serious competitor to Jeserum is even longer-established and carries a comparably exquisite line of linens. *Piazza San Marco.* ☎ *041-5225068. AE, DC, MC, V. Vaporetto: San Marco/Vallaresso. Map p 69.*

Markets
★ **Mercatino dei Miracoli**
Venice's flea market is a monthly affair, and a satisfying place to browse for prints, old jewelry, and other bric-a-brac. *Campo San Canciano and Campo Santa Maria Nova. Second or third weekend of the month. Vaportetto: Ca' d'Oro. Map p 70.*

★★★ **Pescaria and Rialto markets** Venice's fish market (Pescaria) transpires under the arcades of a neo-Gothic hall on the banks of the Grand Canal, and produce markets enliven the adjoining squares. Adding to the general fray are stalls selling souvenirs. Even if you're not in the market for an eel, the goings-on, the mix of locals and tourists, and the centuries-old ambience provide one of the best shows in town. *See* p 21, bullet ⑲. *Daily 7am–1pm. Vaporetto: Rialto. Map p 72.*

Customer buying vegetables in the Rialto Market.

A craftsperson creates carnival masks our of papier-mâché at MondoNovo.

★ **San Leonardo** SAN LEONARDO
Produce vendors set up shop on the banks of a canal, providing a perfect setup shot for shutterbugs looking for everyday Venetian scenes. *Rio Terra San Leonardo. Mon–Sat about 8am–7:30pm. Map p 70.*

★ **Via Giribaldi** CASTELLO Stalls serving the large residential Castello neighborhood sell everything from produce to carving knives. *Via Giribaldi. Mon–Sat 8am–5pm. Open only in winter months. Vaporetto: Arsenale. Map p 69.*

Masks

★★ **Ca' Macana** DORSODURO
See masks being made at one of Venice's most popular stops for carnival wear, and take home a fairly standard mask or a marvelous one-of-a-kind creation. *Calle delle Botteghe.* ☎ *041-5203229. AE, DC, MC, V. Vaporetto: Ca' Rezzonico. Map p 71.*

★ **Il Canovaccio** CASTELLO
Named for a common plot device in *commedia dell'arte*, this shop near San Marco veers from tradition to produce stunning original designs. *Calle delle Bande.* ☎ *041-5210393. AE, MC, V. Vaporetto: San Zaccaria. Map p 69.*

★★ **La Bottega dei Mascareri**
SAN POLO The Boldrin brothers

sell an amazing variety of masks from their crowded shop at the end of the Rialto bridge next to the church of San Giacomo. *Calle de Cristo.* ☎ *041-5223857. AE, MC, V. Vaporetto: Rialto.*

★★★ **MondoNovo** DORSODURO
Venice's largest provider of carnival masks offers creations in papier-mâché that transform the wearer into just about any conceivable persona, from Renaissance dandy to mythological beast. *Rio Terrà Canal.* ☎ *041-5287344. AE, DC, MC, V. Vaporetto: Ca' Rezzonico. Map p 71.*

★★ **Papier Mâché** CASTELLO
Nontraditional masks made by

A wall of colorful carnival masks for sale.

Rolls of colorful handmade paper at the Legatoria Piazzaesi paper shop.

traditional methods are the stock in trade, and many of the elaborate pieces easily pass as works of modern art. *Calle Lunga Santa Maria Formosa.* ☎ *041-5229995. www. papiermache.it. AE, DC, MC, V. Vaporetto: Rialto. Map p 69.*

★★ **Tragicomica** SAN POLO Mask-making is serious business here, and the handmade creations in papier-mâché and leather are gorgeous. *Calle dei Nomboli.* ☎ *041-721102. www.tragicomica.it. AE, DC, MC, V. Vaporetto: San Toma. Map p 72.*

Paper

★ **Biblos** SAN MARCO The several Biblos outlets around Venice sell a nice selection of well-priced picture frames, boxes, and other items made from marbled papers. *Calle Larga XXII Marzo. 041-5210714. AE, MC, V. Vaporetto: Santa Maria del Giglio. Map p 69.*

★★ **Ebru di Federica Novello** SAN MARCO Aficionados of marbled papers will be delighted to see the technique creatively applied to silk scarves and ties, and to a wide range of paper products. *Campo San Stefano.* ☎ *041-5238830. AE,*

DC, MC, V. Vaporetto: Accademia. Map p 69.

★ **Il Papiro** SAN MARCO The Venice outpost of one Italy's most renowned stationers provides well-designed desk accessories to accompany its lines of fine papers. *Calle del Spezier.* ☎ *041-5221202. AE, DC, MC, V. Vaporetto: Santa Maria del Giglio. Map p 69.*

★ **Il Pavone** DORSODURO Items are adorned with the shop's distinctive floral motifs and include beautiful picture frames. *Fondamenta Venier dei Leoni.* ☎ *041-5234517. AE, DC, MC, V. Vaporetto: Accademia.*

★★★ **Legatoria Piazzesi** SAN MARCO At this 150-year-old shop, handmade papers are sold by the piece and fashioned into boxes, address books, and other enticing items. *Campiello Feltrina.* ☎ *041-5221202. www.piazzesi.it. AE, MC, V. Vaporetto: Santa Maria del Giglio. Map p 69.*

★ **Paolo Olbi** SAN MARCO Address books and notepads covered in marbled papers are works of art. *Calle della Mandola, San Marco.* ☎ *041-5285025. MC. Vaporetto: Sant' Angelo. Map p 69.* ●

A Waterside Walk

- **1** Giardini Pubblici to San Marco
- **2** Zattere
- **3** Giudecca

If you're looking for long, unbroken stretches of pavement that are well suited for a fast walk or even a jog, do as the Venetians do: Head to the *fondamenti* (quays or streets) that trace the city's major waterways. Studded with landmarks and abuzz with activity, the following three such locales provide much more than a chance simply to stretch your legs. START: **Take vaporettos 1, 41, or 42 to the Giardini stop**

1 Giardini Pubblici to San Marco. Start with a stroll in the public gardens, then follow the busy *riva* (promenade) that skirts the Bacino di San Marco, changing its name every so often—from Riva dei Sette Martiri (for seven slain World War II partisans) to the Riva degli Schiavoni, named for the Slavic community that founded the nearby Scuola di San Giorgio degli Schiavoni (see p 31, bullet **2**). End the walk

with a flourish, with a saunter through Piazza San Marco. *If you want to keep walking, board a number 1 vaporetto for Salute at the San Marco/Vallaresso stop.*

2 Zattere. Begin at the eastern end of this broad quay, named for the rafts that once unloaded timber here for the construction of Venetian palazzo (see also p 62, bullet **12**). Just beyond the Salute

A bird's-eye view of the Riva degli Schiavoni.

vaporetto stop is the Punta della Dogana—a tip of land adjacent to the Customs house (see p 45, bullet ⑤) that affords breathtaking views of the lagoon, the Grand Canal, and San Marco. As you follow the walk west, your entertainment will be the spectacle of traffic in the Giudecca Canal. The deep-water channel is often jammed with freighters and cruise ships coming and going from the busy port, Stazione Maritima, at the western end of the promenade. *If you want to keep walking, from the San Basilio vaporetto stop at the western end of the Zattere, board a no. 82 boat and cross the canal to the Sant'Eufemia stop on Giudecca.*

③ **Giudecca.** The fondamenta on the northern side of the Giudecca Canal provides a long stretch of pavement well suited for an uninterrupted session of physical exertion—a convenience not lost on the strollers and joggers who make the trip over to the island in good weather. The scenery includes two Palladian churches, Le Zitelle and Il Redentore (see p 46, bullet ①). *From the Zitelle stop, return to San Marco (San Zaccaria stop) on a no. 82 boat.*

Islands in the Lagoon

You'll find a Venetian version of country living on two adjacent islands, **Sant'Erasmo** and **Vignole**, where the main business is growing vegetables for the city markets. Sant'Erasmo is especially famous for its purple artichokes, *carciofi violetto*. Indeed, the thing to do on both islands is to simply stroll along the few roads and admire fields of these and other produce—along with some pleasing views over the lagoon. Take vaporetto 13 to both islands; disembark at the Chiesa stop on Sant'Erasmo.

The Lido

1 Gran Viale Santa Maria
   Elisabetta & the seafront
2 San Nicolò
3 Malamocco
4 Alberoni
5 Pellestrina

This stretch of sand, 12km (7½ miles) long and barely 1km (½ mile) wide, separates the Adriatic from the lagoon and is where Venetians come to play—along the lines of swimming, golfing, riding bikes, and playing tennis. The Lido is also a pleasant place to walk on attractive, shady streets or along the miles of sand beaches. As you explore you can try to conjure up a bit of Belle Epoque–style decadence, a la Thomas Mann's novella *Death in Venice,* but these days the Lido is more a bourgeois suburb than an elite playground.

START: **Take vaporettos 1, 41, 42, 51, 52, or 53 to Lido**

Sailboats on a Lido beach.

1 Gran Viale Santa Maria Elisabetta & the seafront. The Lido's main street runs between the Lido vaporetto stop at Piazzale Maria Elisabetta to Piazzale Bucontoro on the seafront. *Fin de siècle* luxury is in evidence, especially around the extravagant Hotel des Bains and Excelsior Palace on the Lungomare Marconi, just south of Piazzale Bucontoro, as is plenty of idleness: The private cabana-backed beaches are packed with hotel guests and Venetians who pay a handsome price to pass a summer day relaxing in the sun. *To reach Piazzale Bucontoro and the seafront from Piazzale Maria Elisabetta, walk down Gran Viale (about 15 min); or take buses 11, B, or V.*

2 San Nicolò. This town at the northern tip of the Lido has a long history, with a church founded in the 11th century, a 14th-century Jewish cemetery, and the offshore, 16th-century Fortezza di Sant'Andrea, built to defend the Porto di Lido, the main sea entrance to the lagoon. Of more interest to many visitors are the miles of public beaches that surround the town. *Buses A and B run*

Beach cabanas on the Lido.

The Jewish cemetery at St. Nicolò.

from Piazzale Maria Elisabetta to San Nicolò, about 1.5km (1 mile). Guided tours of the cemetery on Sun, 2:30pm (☎ 041-715359).

3 Malamocco. The most attractive community on the Lido is a quaint fishing village surrounding a pretty campo. Once a bustling port for the inland city of Padua, Malamocco was swept away in a tidal wave in 1106 and rebuilt in its present guise in the 15th century. *Buses 11, B, and V run from Piazzale Maria Elisabetta to Malamocco, about 5km (3 miles).*

4 Alberoni. At the edge of the southernmost settlement on the Lido are the greens of the only golf course in Venice. The town's attractive beaches are backed by dunes and pine forests and are especially popular with gay men. *Bus 11 runs from Piazzale Maria Elisabetta to Alberoni, about 12km (7½ miles).*

5 Pellistrina. This island, separated from the Lido by a narrow channel, is where many Venetians prefer to spend a day at the beach. The 10km-long (6-mile) strip of scrubby vegetation is no more than a sand bar, with two attractive fishing communities, San Pietro in Volta and Pellestrina. *Bus 11 runs from Piazzale Maria Elisabetta to Pellistrina, about 13km (8 miles).* ●

Getting Active on the Lido

Golf. Circolo Golf Venezia, Strada Vecchia 1, Alberoni-Lido. ☎ 041-731-3333. www.circologolfvenezia.it. Apr–Sept, Tues–Sun 8am–8pm, Oct–Mar, Tues–Sun 8:30am–6pm. 55€ weedays, 70€ weekends; cart rental, 35€ for 18 holes. This 18-hole, par 72 course is the only place to play golf in Venice, and is one of Italy's top courses.

Bicycle rental. Giardin Anna Valli, Piazzale Santa Maria Elisabetta, Lido. ☎ 041-2760005. May–Oct, 8am–8pm. 2.60€ an hour, 8€ a day. The flat terrain of the Lido is perfect for cycling.

Tennis. Tennis Club Ca' Del Moro. Via Ferrucio Parri 6, Lido. ☎ 041-770965. Mon–Sat 8:30am–8:30pm, Sun 8:30am–8pm. 8.50€ per hour. One of the Lido's best public tennis facilities also has a pool and a gym.

Dining **Best Bets**

Best **Deep-Dish Pizza**
★★ Acqua Pazza $$–$$$ *Campo Sant'Angelo, San Marco* (p 97)

Best **Place to Have a Panino with a View**
★★ Algiubagiò $ *Fondamenta Nuove, Cannaregio* (p 98)

Best **Vegetarian Meal**
★★ Alla Zucca $ *Ponte del Megio, Santa Croce* (p 99)

Best **Hot Chocolate**
★★★ Antica Pasticceria Inguanotto $ *Ponte del Lovo, San Marco* (p 99)

Best **Place to Get a Whiff of Student Life**
★★ Caffé dei Frari $ *Fondamenta dei Frari, San Polo* (p 100)

Best **Stop for Carnivores**
★★★ Dalla Marisa $ *Fondamenta San Giobbe, Cannaregio* (p 101)

Best **Atmosphere for a Quick Bite**
★★ Do Mori $ *Calle dei Do Mori, San Polo* (p 102)

Best **(Arguable) Gelato**
★★★ Gelateria Nico $ *Fondamenta Zattere, Dorsoduro* (p 103)

Best **Choice for an Affordable Seafood Meal**
★★★ Corte Sconta $$ *Calle del Pestrin, Castello* (p 101)

Best **Old-World Atmosphere**
★★ Gran Caffé Ristorante Quadri $$$ *Piazza San Marco, San Marco* (p 103)

Best **Place to See the Rich & Famous & the Rich & Not So Famous**
★★ Harry's Bar $$$$ *Calle Vallaresso, San Marco* (p 103)

Best **Place to Drop a Bundle while Enjoying the View**
★★ Harry's Dolci $$$$ *Fondamenta San Biagio, Giudecca* (p 103)

Best **Place to Propose Marriage**
★★★ Locanda Cipriani $$$$ *Piazza Santa Fosca, Torcello* (p 104)

Best **Place to Take a Break from Italian Cooking**
★★ Mirai $$ *Lista di Spagna, Cannaregio* (p 105)

Best **(Arguable) Meal in Town**
★★★ Osteria da Fiore $$$$ *Calle delle Scaleter, San Polo* (p 106)

Best **Place to Have a Pastry & a Cappuccino**
★★★ Rosa Salva $ *Campo Santi Giovanni e Paolo, Castello* (p 106)

Fresh octopus is sold in the daily fish market in the Campo di Rialto.

San Marco & Castello **Dining**

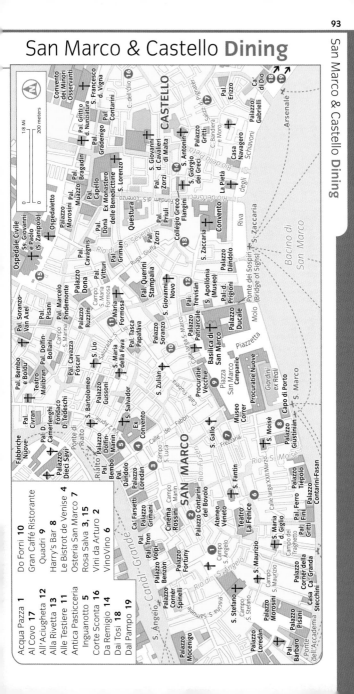

Acqua Pazza **1**
Al Covo **17**
All'Aciugheta **12**
Alla Rivetta **13**
Alle Testiere **11**
Antica Pasticceria
Inguanotto **5**
Corte Sconta **16**
Da Remigio **14**
Dai Tosi **18**
Dal Pampo **19**

Do Forni **10**
Gran Caffè Ristorante
Quadri **9**
Harry's Bar **8**
Le Bistrot de Venise **4**
Osteria San Marco **7**
Rosa Salva **3, 15**
Vini da Arturo **2**
VinoVino **6**

Cannaregio Dining

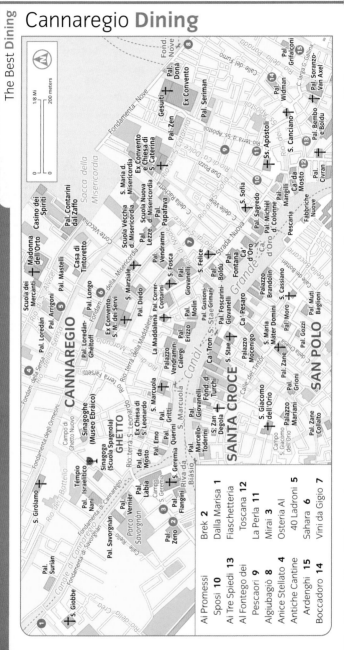

Dorsoduro **Dining**

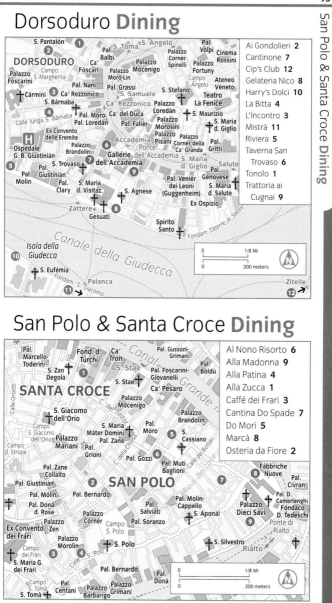

Ai Gondolieri **2**
Cantinone **7**
Cip's Club **12**
Gelateria Nico **8**
Harry's Dolci **10**
La Bitta **4**
L'Incontro **3**
Mistrà **11**
Riviera **5**
Taverna San
  Trovaso **6**
Tonolo **1**
Trattoria ai
  Cugnai **9**

San Polo & Santa Croce **Dining**

Al Nono Risorto **6**
Alla Madonna **9**
Alla Patina **4**
Alla Zucca **1**
Caffé dei Frari **3**
Cantina Do Spade **7**
Do Mori **5**
Marcà **2**
Osteria da Fiore **2**

The Islands **Dining**

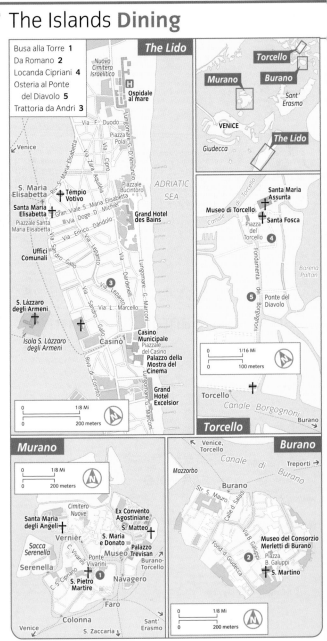

Busa alla Torre **1**
Da Romano **2**
Locanda Cipriani **4**
Osteria al Ponte
del Diavolo **5**
Trattoria da Andri **3**

Venice Restaurants A to Z

★★ Acqua Pazza SAN MARCO
NEAPOLITAN This perennially busy indoor-outdoor pizzeria-ristorante is a good place to come with companions with varying appetites and bankrolls: You can dine simply and moderately on the delicious, deep-dish Neapolitan pies or sample one of the many fish and seafood dishes inspired by the southern city. *Campo Sant'Angelo.* ☎ *041-2770688. Entrees 9€–25€. AE, DC, MC, V. Open Tues–Sun noon–3pm, 7–11pm. Vaporetto: Sant'Angelo. Map p 93.*

★★★Ai Gondolieri DORSODURO
ITALIAN In this charming old inn alongside a canal, the freshest vegetables from the farmland surrounding the lagoon augment a rare offering in Venice—a wide selection of meat dishes, concentrating on such seasonal favorites as duck and venison. *Ponte del Formager.* ☎ *041-5286396. Entrees 20€–30€. MC, V. Open Wed–Mon noon–2:30pm, 7–9:30pm. Vaporetto: Accademia. Map p 95.*

★★ Ai Promessi Sposi
CANNAREGIO *ITALIAN* This is a great place to sample *cicheti,* the Venetian version of tapas—rice balls, fried olives, marinated seafood, grilled vegetables, and on and on. The simple pasta and meat dishes are excellent and well priced, too. *Calle dell'Oca.* ☎ *041-5228609. Entrees 7€–10€. No credit cards. Open Thurs–Tues 10am–10pm. Vaporetto: Fondamente Nuove. Map p 94.*

★★ Ai Tre Spiedi CANNAREGIO
VENETIAN/ITALIAN On offer in this small, inviting room are a fine selection of Venetian favorites, including some of the city's freshest fish and seafood, as well as meat and pastas dishes from beyond the lagoon. *Salizzada San Canciano.* ☎ *041-5208035.*

Cafe patrons enjoying lunch on a Venice piazza.

Entrees 10€–20€. AE, MC, V. Open Tues–Sat noon–3pm; Tues–Sun 7–10pm. Vaporetto: Rialto. Map p 94.

★★★ Al Covo CASTELLO
VENETIAN/SEAFOOD Only the freshest fish and seafood are used in the delightful preparations; I particularly recommend a memorable pasta with scallops. The appealing surroundings extend into a pretty garden. *Campiello della Pescaria.* ☎ *041-5223812. Entrees 12€–20€. No credit cards. Open Fri–Tues 12:30–2pm, 7:30–10pm. Vaporetto: Arsenale. Map p 93.*

★★★ Al Fontego dei Pescaori
CANNAREGIO *VENETIAN/SEAFOOD* Not too far from the Rialto fish markets, this chic eatery puts a new spin on Venetian seafood classics with the addition of fresh seasonal produce and creative spices. Meat dishes are approached with the same refreshing touch. *Sottoportego del Tagliapietra.* ☎ *041-5200538. Entrees 15€–30€.*

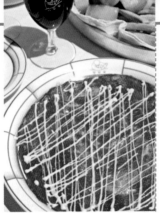

A classic carpaccio (raw beef with a dressing), an original Venice creation.

AE, DC, MC, V. Open Mon, Wed–Sun noon–2:30pm, 7–10pm. Vaporetto: Ca d'Oro. Map p 94.

★★ Algiubagiò CANNAREGIO *CAFE* The terrace provides a view of the busy comings and goings at the vaporetto stop, the departure point for the islands. Before boarding, fortify yourself with a sandwich or even a dish of pasta, or grab a slice of pizza from the adjoining counter to take with you. *Fondamenta Nuove.* ☎ *041-5227949. Entrees 3€–8€. AE, DC, MC, V. Open daily 6:30am–midnight. Vaporetto: Fondamenta Nove. Map p 94.*

★★ All'Aciugheta CASTELLO *VENETIAN/ITALIAN Cicheti—* Venetian snacks such as small meatballs and stuffed peppers—are the specialty here, served with a vast selection of wine. Pizzas, pastas, and other standard fare are also available. *Campo Santi Filippo e Giacomo.* ☎ *041-5224292. Entrees 9€–15€. MC, V. Open daily 11:30am–10:30pm. Vaporetto: San Zaccaria. Map p 93.*

★★★ Alla Madonna SAN POLO *VENETIAN/SEAFOOD* As befits a location near the Rialto fish market, this clamorous, charming trattoria serves the freshest fish and seafood available, which arrives at the table in such classic Venetian preparations as a rich *zuppa di pesce* (fish soup) and *vermicelli al nero di seppia* (vermicelli with a sauce of cuttlefish ink). *Calle della Madonna.* ☎ *041-5223824. Entrees 9€–15€. AE, MC, V. Open Thurs–Tues noon–3pm, 7–10pm. Closed Jan, 2 weeks in Aug. Vaporetto: Rialto. Map p 95.*

★★ Alla Patina SAN POLO *VENETIAN/WINE BAR* The name refers to the specialty of the house, fried potatoes served as a quick snack. Many other tasty morsels are also on hand at the bar, and heartier fish and pasta dishes are served at the tables. *Ponte San Polo.* ☎ *041-5237238. Entrees 7€–15€. AE, DC, MC, V. Open Mon–Sat 9:30–2:30pm, 5–10pm; meals Mon–Sat noon–2:30pm, 6:30–10pm. Vaporetto: San Tomà. Map p 95.*

★★ Alla Rivetta CASTELLO *VENETIAN/ITALIAN* The proximity of San Marco and the swanky Hotel Daniele doesn't deter from a casual neighborhood atmosphere—or the good value of one of the best-prepared *fritto misto* (mixed fry) in

Inside the trattoria Alla Madonna.

Preparing Venetian prawns

town. *Ponte San Provolo.* ☎ 041-5287302. *Entrees 9€–19€. AE, MC, V. Open Tues–Sun 10am–10pm. Vaporetto: San Zaccaria. Map p 93.*

★★ **Alla Zucca** SANTA CROCE *ITALIAN/VEGETARIAN* The emphasis here is on vegetarian cooking, which, given the bounty of the Veneto, is not to be overlooked; even so, deftly prepared fish and lamb dishes also appear on the menu. *Ponte del Megio.* ☎ 041-5241570. *Entrees 9€–11€. AE, DC, MC, V. Open Mon–Sat 12:30–2:30pm, 7–10:30pm. Vaporetto: San Stae. Map p 95.*

★★★ **Alle Testiere** CASTELLO *VENETIAN/SEAFOOD* One of Venice's trendiest and most hyped restaurants well deserves its fame, serving aromatic seafood dishes, fine wines, and excellent cheeses in causal-chic surroundings. *Calle del Mondo Novo.* ☎ 041-5227220. *Entrees 15€–25€. MC, V. Open Tues–Sun noon–2pm, 7–10:30pm (two seatings, at 7 & 9:15pm). Vaporetto: Rialto. Map p 93.*

★ **Al Nono Risorto** SANTA CROCE *ITALIAN/PIZZA* The pizza's fine if not exceptional, and the same goes for the perfectly passable traditional pasta and meat and fish fare; what's exceptional is the lovely garden, a fine place to idle away a summer evening. *Sottoportico di*

Siora Bettina. ☎ 041-5241169. *Entrees 7€–12€. No credit cards. Open Fri–Tues 7–11pm. Vaporetto: San Stae. Map p 95.*

★★★ **Anice Stellato** CANNAREGIO *VENETIAN* The simple, laid-back decor in the small beamed rooms and reasonable prices might not prepare you for what's coming your way here: exceptionally good preparations of fish and such classics as *fegato all veneziana* (calf's liver, Venetian style, sautéed with onions). Start with an assortment of *cicheti* (morsels of fish) and other snacks served from the bar in front. *Fondamenta della Sensa.* ☎ 041-5238153. *Entrees 12€–15€. MC, V. Open Wed–Sun 12:30–2pm, 7:30–10pm. Closed Aug. Vaporetto: Fondamente Nove. Map p 94.*

★★★ **Antica Pasticceria Inguanotto** SAN MARCO *CAFE* This Venetian institution accompanies its fine pastries with delicious hot chocolate and excellent coffee. *Ponte del Lovo.* ☎ 041-5208439. *2€–4€. MC, V. Open June–Sept Mon–Sat 8am–8:30pm; Oct–May Mon–Sat 8am–8:30pm, Sun noon–8pm. Vaporetto: Rialto. Map p 93.*

★★ **Antiche Cantine Ardenghi** CANNAREGIO *VENETIAN/SEAFOOD* The food is typically Venetian, with a small but flavorful selection of seafood dishes made fresh daily; but the experience—from the unmarked location to the quirky patrons to the bottomless carafes of house wine—may be unlike anything you've experienced before. *Calle della Testa.* ☎ *041-5237691. Entrees 50€ prix-fixe. No credit cards. Open Tues–Sat 8pm (one seating). Vaporetto: Fondamente Nove. Map p 94.*

★★★ **Boccadoro** CANNAREGIO *VENETIAN/SEAFOOD* These intimate and relaxed surroundings are for many Venetians the best place in town to enjoy fresh, inventive seafood dishes. *Pesce crudo* (raw fish) selections feature sashimi of the freshest and perfectly spiced Adriatic fish, and mussels, clams, and shrimp appear in elegant pasta and risotto dishes. *Campiello Widman.* ☎ *041-5211021. Entrees 15€–30€. AE, DC, MC, V. Open Tues–Sun 12:30–2:30pm, 8–11:30pm. Vaporetto: Fondamente Nuove. Map p 94.*

★ **Brek** CANNAREGIO *ITALIAN* Even if cafeteria-style dining isn't on your Venetian culinary agenda, you might enjoy a stop or two at this attractive outlet of a highly regarded Italian chain, located on Strada Nuovo, the main pedestrian route to San Marco. The selections of cold meats, pastas, cheeses, and salads

A basket of fresh tomatoes awaits preparation.

Stracciatella cheese roulade.

are impressive and provide an excellent and affordable light meal. *Lista di Spagna.* ☎ *041-2440158. Entrees 5€–8€. AE, DC, MC, V. Open daily 10am–10pm. Vaporetto: Ferrovia. Map p 94.*

★★★ **Busa alla Torre** MURANO *VENETIAN/SEAFOOD* Escape the island's glass-shop craze and take a seat in the pleasant dining room or on the terrace beneath the bell tower—the welcome respite includes an excellent meal, featuring such specialties as *ravioli di pesce.* *Campo Santo Stefano.* ☎ *041-739662. Entrees 15€–30€. AE, MC, V. Open daily noon–3:30pm. Vaporetto: Colonna. Map p 96.*

★★ **Caffé dei Frari** SAN POLO *CAFE* This cozy nook is popular with students from the university and provides a nice refuge for weary visitors to the nearby Frari and Scuola Grande di San Rocco (see p 32, bullet ⑨). *Fondamenta dei Frari.* ☎ *041-5241877. Entrees 3€–6€. No credit cards. Open Mon–Fri 8am–midnight; Sat 5pm–midnight; Sun 5–9pm. Vaporetto: San Tomà. Map p 95.*

★★★ Cantina Do Spade SAN
POLO VENETIAN/WINE BAR Dating from the 15th century and serving a clientele that has included Casanova, this atmosphere-soaked wine bar can indeed call itself a Venice institution. You can dine well on the *cicheti*—snacks of fried calamari and other morsels—and the fixed-price menus served at the few tables offer tasty and affordable full meals. *Sotto-portego do Spade.* ☎ 041-5210574. Entrees 7€–10€. AE, MC, V. Open daily 9am–3pm, 5–11pm. Vaporetto: Rialto. Map p 95.

★★ Cantinone DORSODURO
WINE BAR This little wine bar makes large and delicious panini that, along with a tempting array of crostini topped with cheeses and vegetables, can easily suffice for lunch or a light evening meal. Whatever morsel you choose should be accompanied by a glass of the chilled Prosecco. *Ponte San Trovaso.* ☎ 041-5230034. Entrees 12€–17€. No credit cards. Open Mon–Sat 8:30am–8:30pm. Vaporetto: Accademia. Map p 95.

★★ Cip's Club GIUDECCA
VENETIAN/SEAFOOD Is the view worth the price? Sitting on the wooden terrace overlooking the Giudecca Canal and San Marco is certainly a treat. If the hefty tab for such house specialties as *mazzan-colle* (prawns) with capers is going to break the bank, settle for just a first course, such as the delicious risotto with scallops and baby artichokes—or, for that matter, a cocktail at sunset. *Hotel Cipriani.* ☎ 041-5207744. Entrees 30€–45€. AE, DC, MC, V. Open daily noon–3:30pm, 7–11pm. Vaporetto: Zitelle. Map p 95.

★★★ Corte Sconta CASTELLO
VENETIAN/SEAFOOD One of the top choices in town for fresh, deftly prepared seafood, much of which comes to the table in delectable pasta dishes and risottos. Reserve well in advance, and request a table in the namesake courtyard. *Calle del Pestrin.* ☎ 041-5227024. Entrees 12€–20€. MC, V. Open Tues–Sat 12:30–2pm, 7–10pm. Vaporetto: Giardini. Map p 93.

★ Dai Tosi CASTELLO ITALIAN
Something Venice has all too few of—a friendly neighborhood pizzeria, complete with a rear garden. Handy for the (Biennale), which is held in the adjacent public gardens. *Secco Marina, Castello.* ☎ 041-5237102. Entrees 8€–16€. MC, V. Open Mon, Tues, Thurs noon–2pm; Fri–Sun noon–2pm, 7–9:30pm. Vaporetto: Giardini. Map p 93.

★★★ Dalla Marisa CANNAREGIO
ITALIAN No serious carnivore will want to leave Venice without enjoying at least one meal at this small osteria near the Ponte di Tre Archi (in fact, you can see this landmark from the tables out front alongside the canal). Old-fashioned ways still hold sway in the kitchen, which sends out traditional preparations of *osso buco* (braised veal shanks), *tripa* (tripe), and other classics. *Fonda-menta San Giobbe.* ☎ 041-720211. Entrees 9€–14€. No credit cards.

Agnello aranzato, *roasted lamb in an aranzato sauce, a classic from Le Bistrot de Venise.*

Open Tues, Thurs–Sat noon–2:30pm, 8–9:15pm; Sat–Mon noon–2:30pm only. Closed Aug. Vaporetto: Tre Archi. Map p 94.

★★ **Dal Pampo** SANT' ELENA *VENETIAN/ITALIAN* The official name is Osteria Sant'Elena, but everyone knows this busy trattoria in the out-of-the-way Sant'Elena neighborhood as "Pampo's Place." Pasta dishes, *fritto misto* (mixed fry, here of seafood), and other traditional favorites, along with bar snacks, satisfy a crowd of regulars. *Calle Generale Chinotto.* ☎ *041-5208419. Entrees 7€–15€. AE, MC, V. Open Mon–Wed, Fri–Sun noon– 2:30pm, 7:30–9pm. Vaporetto: Sant'Elena. Map p 93.*

★★ **Da Remigio** CASTELLO *VENETIAN/SEAFOOD* What the busy premises lack in charm is more than compensated by the mostly seafood menu, expertly prepared and featuring such Adriatic staples as *fritto misto* and fish caught that day and simply grilled. *Salizada dei Greci.* ☎ *041-5230089. Entrees 8€–16€. AE, DC, MC, V. Open Fri–Tues 12:30–2pm, 7:30–10pm. Vaporetto: Arsenale. Map p 93.*

★★ **Da Romano** BURANO *VENETIAN/SEAFOOD* Such specialties as a simple risotto flavored with

fish broth are memorable, but Romano banks on its celebrated clientele—some famous, others of an artistic bent whose paintings cover every inch of the walls. *Via Galuppi.* ☎ *041-730030. Entrees 15€–30€. AE, DC, MC, V. Open Wed–Mon noon–3:30pm, 7–9:30pm. Vaporetto: Burano. Map p 96.*

★★★ **Do Forni** SAN MARCO *VENETIAN/INTERNATIONAL* The former bakery of the monastery of San Zaccaria now serves excellent Venetian seafood specialties in two dining rooms, one (the more appealing) rustic and whitewashed, the other upholstered and paneled like a carriage car on the *Orient Express.* *Calle dei Specchieri.* ☎ *041-5232148. Entrees 13€–24€. AE, DC, MC, V. Open daily noon– 3pm, 7–11pm. Vaporetto: San Marco/ Vallaresso. Map p 93.*

★★ **Do Mori** SAN POLO *VENETIAN/ WINE BAR* This dark, battered-looking old place situated in the midst of the Rialto markets has been dispensing wine and snacks for some 6 centuries and still packs in an appreciative crowd of regulars. By tradition, Venetians pop in to places like this for a before-dinner or late-night snack, but the delicious little sandwiches and tidbits of fish, meats,

Getateria Nico.

and cheeses pass nicely for a meal when you've had your fill of more formal fare. *Calle dei Do Mori.* ☎ 041-5225401. *Entrees 2€–3€. No credit cards. Open Mon–Sat 8:30am–8:30pm. Vaporetto: Rialto. Map p 95.*

★★ Fiaschetteria Toscana

CANNAREGIO *VENETIAN/ITALIAN* The name refers to the Tuscan wines and oils once stored and sold from the now-elegant premises. These days the offerings are such Venetian specialties as grilled sardines and *fegato alla veneziana* (calf's liver sautéed in oil and spices). The flawless preparations and excellent service provide a memorable dining experience that may well be worth the splurge. *Salizzada San Giovanni Grisostomo, Cannaregio.* ☎ 041-5285281. *Entrees 12€–35€. AE, DC, MC, V. Open Mon 7:30–10:30pm; Wed–Sun 12:30–2:30pm, 7:30–10:30pm. Vaporetto: Rialto. Map p 94.*

★★★ Gelateria Nico DORSO-

DURO *CAFE* Pizzas and sandwiches are available on a terrace overlooking the Giudecca Canal, but the draw for most patrons is the terrific gelato made on the premises. *Fondamenta Zattere.* ☎ 041-5225293. *Entrees 3€–8€. No credit cards. Open June–Sept daily 7:30am–11:30pm; Oct–May daily 9:30am–1pm. Vaporetto: Zattere. Map p 95.*

★★ Gran Caffè Ristorante

Quadri SAN MARCO *VENETIAN/ INTERNATIONAL* It's easy to be swayed by the swank mirrored and silk-festooned interior of this elegant dining room above one of Europe's most famous cafes (p 114), but the food is memorable, too—and not as expensive as the surroundings suggest. Be sure to save room for the house-made gelato of amaretto mousse and meringue. *Piazza San Marco.* ☎ 041-5222105. www.quadri venice.com. *Entrees 19€–24€. AE,*

Carpaccio, first created by Arrigo Cipriani of Harry's Bar in Venice, is here served with beets and goat cheese.

DC, MC, V. Open Apr–Oct daily 12:15–2pm, 7:15–10:15pm; Nov–Mar Tues–Sun 12:15–2pm, 7:15–10:15pm. Vaporetto: San Marco/Vallaresso. Map p 93.

★★ Harry's Bar SAN MARCO

VENETIAN/INTERNATIONAL A favorite for many, way too overpriced and generic for others. But everyone agrees that Harry's wafer-thin carpaccio (invented here) and scampi are memorable classics. You may be just as happy settling for a Bellini in the bar (p 114). The frothy concoction of peach juice and sparkling wine was invented here. *Calle Vallaresso.* ☎ 041-5285777. *Entrees 36€–45€. AE, DC, MC, V. Open noon–3pm, 7–11pm. Vaporetto: San Marco/Vallaresso. Map p 93.*

★★ Harry's Dolci GIUDECCA

VENETIAN/SEAFOOD At this offshoot of Harry's Bar, you can't claim to occupy a table once occupied by the likes of Ernest Hemingway or Orson Welles, but there are compensations—the trip out to the Giudecca is an adventure, the views from the terrace on the Giudecca

Canal are stupendous, and the fare, including such trademark Harry's dishes as carpaccio and seafood risottos, is just as good as that served at the original. *Fondamenta San Biagio.* ☎ *041-5224844. Entrees 30€–45€. AE, DC, MC, V. Open Apr–Oct Wed–Mon noon–3pm, 7–10:30pm. Vaporetto: Sant'Eufemia. Map p 95.*

★★ La Bitta DORSODURO

ITALIAN The wide choice of meat dishes, along with the warm welcome, sets this inviting room apart from many other Venetian eateries. Local produce is the ingredient of delicious salads, and duck and rabbit are among the hearty main-course offerings. *Calle Lunga San Barnaba.* ☎ *041-5230531. Entrees 12€–17€. AE, DC, MC, V. Open Thurs–Sun noon–2pm, 7–11 pm. Vaporetto: Ca' Rezzonico. Map p 95.*

★★ La Perla CANNAREGIO

PIZZA/ITALIAN Perla bakes an exquisite pizza, a fact not lost on the hordes of students and locals who pack into the undistinguished but always lively surroundings. *Rio Terà dei Franceschi.* ☎ *041-5285175. Entrees 7€–10€. MC, V. Open Mon–Sat noon–2pm, 7–9:45pm (closed Aug). Vaporetto: Ca' d'Oro. Map p 94.*

★★ Le Bistrot de Venise

SAN MARCO *VENETIAN/SEAFOOD* It may be a crowded stop on the tourist trail, but the kitchen does justice to such Venetian classics as linguine with lobster and lasagna with red mullet. *Calle dei Fabbri.* ☎ *041-5236651. Entrees 14€–22€. AE, MC, V. Open daily noon–1am. Vaporetto: Rialto. Map p 93.*

★★★ L'Incontro DORSODURO

SARDINIAN A Sardinian chef brings the hearty fare of his island to Venice, serving roast rabbit, suckling pig, and some of the finest steaks in town, accompanied, of course, by Sardinian wines. *Rio Terà Canal.* ☎ *041-5222404. Entrees 15€–20€. AE, DC, MC, V. Open Tues 7:30– 10:30pm, Wed–Sun 12:30–2:30pm, 7:30–10:30pm. Closed Jan. Vaporetto: Ca' Rezzonico. Map p 95.*

★★★ Locanda Cipriani TORCELLO

VENETIAN/SEAFOOD For many devotees, the sole purpose of a trip to this enchanting island in the lagoon is a meal on the shady terrace of this elegantly rustic hotel. The atmosphere wins out over the food, however, which stays in the predictable range of *vitello tonnato* (poached veal with a sauce of tuna and capers), seafood pastas, and grilled fish. To add one more

The restaurant Le Bistrot de Venise.

The patio at Locanda Cipriani, on the island of Torcello.

ingredient to a romantic evening here, arrange your transport in the hotel's private launch (about 20€ a person). *Piazza Santa Fosca.* ☎ 041-730150. *Entrees 25€–40€. AE, DC, MC, V. Open Wed–Mon noon–3:30pm, 7–9pm. Closed Jan. Vaporetto: Torcello. Map p 96.*

★★★ **Marcà** SAN POLO *CAFE*
A crowded room dispenses an assortment of panini, crostini, and other Venetian-style fast food to neighborhood shoppers and workers. *Campo Cesare Battisti. Entrees 3€–6€. No credit cards. Open Mon–Fri 7am–3pm, 6–9:30pm; Sat 7am–3pm. Vaporetto: Rialto. Map p 95.*

★★ **Mirai** CANNAREGIO *JAPANESE*
It stands to reason that Venice's bountiful fresh fish and seafood are ideal for sushi and sashimi creations, and here they are—served in attractive surroundings that fuse Venetian and Asian chic. *Lista di Spagna.* ☎ 041-2206000. *Entrees 10€–25€. AE, DC, MC, V. Open Tues–Sun 7:30–11:30pm. Vaporetto: Ferrovia. Map p 94.*

★★ **Mistrà** GIUDECCA *VENETIAN*
A ship-worker's canteen now offers such culinary delights as *sarde in saor* (pickled sardines) to those

willing to find their way to the backwaters of the Giudecca. A set-price lunch is a real bargain at 12€. *Off Calle San Giacomo.* ☎ 041-5220743. *Entrees 10€–25€. AE, DC, MC, V. Open Mon noon–3:30pm; Wed–Sun noon–3:30pm, 7:30–10:30pm. Vaporetto: Redentore. Map p 95.*

★★ **Osteria Al 40 Ladroni**
CANNAREGIO *VENETIAN/SEAFOOD*
The freshest fish, simply prepared, keeps a crowd of regulars happy—especially when they're lucky enough to snag one of the outdoor tables next to the canal. *Fondamenta della Sensa.* ☎ 041-715736. *Entrees 9€–20€. DC, MC, V. Open Tues–Sun noon–2:30pm, 7–10:30pm. Vaporetto: San Marcuola. Map p 94.*

★★★ **Osteria al Ponte del Diavolo** TORCELLO *VENETIAN/ SEAFOOD* The neighbor of Locanda Cipriani on Torcello very capably plays a quieter role, offering excellent fish and seafood specialties served in attractive, rustic rooms, on a patio, and in a garden. *Fondamenta Borgognoni.* ☎ 041-730401. *Entrees 15€–30€. AE, DC, MC, V. Open Thurs–Tues noon–3:30pm, 7–9pm. Vaporetto: Torcello. Map p 96.*

A diner peruses a book in the small, classic dining room at Osteria da Fiore.

★★★ Osteria da Fiore SAN POLO

VENETIAN/SEAFOOD The Martin family has earned a Michelin star along with a reputation for serving the best food in Venice, for offerings that include a vast selection of seafood antipasti, elegant pasta dishes, and such flavorful entrees as sea bass in balsamic vinegar. Behind the modest facade is a small, luxurious dining room that is a prime gathering spot for the rich and sometimes famous. *Calle delle Scaleter.* ☎ *041-721308. Entrees 20€–40€. AE, DC, MC, V. Open Tues–Sat 12:30–2:30pm, 7:30–10:30pm. Closed Aug. Vaporetto: San Stae. Map p 95.*

★★★ Osteria San Marco SAN

MARCO *ITALIAN/WINE BAR* This snazzy new wine bar does justice to its upscale San Marco neighborhood, serving a nice selection of *cicheti* (tapaslike snacks) at the bar and deftly prepared fare in the chicly austere dining room, where the emphasis is on fresh fish and local produce. *Frezzeria.* ☎ *041-5285242. Entrees 9€–25€. AE, MC, V. Open Mon–Sat 12:30–2:30pm, 7:30–10pm. Vaporetto: San Marco/Vallaresso. Map p 93.*

★★ Riviera DORSODURO

VENETIAN/SEAFOOD Accomplished cooking and colorful views of the busy Giudecca Canal are a winning combination in this tiny dining room and its large terrace. This is a perfect retreat for a warm evening and offers a small but well-chosen menu of meat and fish dishes. *Zattere.* ☎ *041-5227621. Entrees 18€–24€. MC, V. Open Tues–Sun noon–2:30pm, 7:30–10:30pm. Vaporetto: Zattere. Map p 95.*

★★★ Rosa Salva CASTELLO *CAFE*

A delicious cappuccino comes with a view of one of the most beautiful squares in Venice (see p 41, bullet ④), as well as a nice assortment of pastries, sandwiches, and delicious gelato made on the premises. *Campo Santi Giovanni e Paolo.* ☎ *041-5227949. Entrees 2€–4€. No credit cards. Open Mon–Tues, Thurs–Sat 7:30am–8:30pm; Sun 8:30am–8:30pm. Vaporetto: Fondamenta Nove. Branch at Campo San Luca, San Marco.* ☎ *041-5225385. Map p 93.*

★★ Sahara CANNAREGIO *MIDDLE*

EASTERN The Syrian-Egyptian offerings range from kabobs to couscous and provide an exotic break from Italian fare. A boat moored next to the outdoor tables is sometimes a stage for classical ensembles, and a belly dancer winds through the dining room on Saturday evenings. *Fondamenta della Misericordia.* ☎ *041-721077. Entrees 7€–10€. MC, V. Open Mon–Fri 7pm–2am; Sat, Sun noon–2:30pm, 7–2pm. Vaporetto: San Marcuola. Map p 94.*

★★ Taverna San Trovaso
DORSODURO *VENETIAN* A cozy setting of paneled walls and brick-vaulted ceiling provides just the place to enjoy such heart-warming Venetian classics as *fritto misti* (here, a mix of fried seafood) or grilled fish. *Fondamenta Priuli.* ☎ *041-5203703. Entrees 8€–16€. AE, DC, MC, V. Open Tues–Sun noon–2:30pm, 7–9:30pm. Vaporetto: Rialto. Map p 95.*

★★★ Tonolo DORSODURO *CAFE* A fine selection of cakes makes this elegant little place a popular stop in the Campo Santa Margherita neighborhood. *Calle San Pantalon.* ☎ *041-5237209. Entrees 2€–4€. No credit cards. Open Tues–Sat 7:45am–8:30pm; Sun 7:45am–1pm. Vaporetto: San Tomà. Map p 95.*

★★ Trattoria ai Cugnai DORSO-DURO *VENETIAN* Homemade pastas and soups and nicely prepared versions of such Venetian standards as *fegato* (calf's liver) make this informal eatery a pleasant stop for visitors to the nearby Accademia and Guggenheim galleries. *Calle Nuova Sant'Agnese.* ☎ *041-5289238. Entrees 6€–18€. MC, V. Open Tues–Sun 12:30–3pm, 7–10:30pm. Vaporetto: Accademia. Map p 95.*

★★ Trattoria da Andri LIDO *VENETIAN/ SEAFOOD* Superbly prepared fish dishes, served on a delightful terrace, ensure a pleasant meal on the Lido. *Via Lepanto.* ☎ *041-5265482. Entrees 15€–30€. AE, DC, MC, V. Open Wed–Sun noon–3:30pm ,ad 7–9:30pm. Vaporetto: Lido. Map p 96.*

★★ Vini da Arturo SAN MARCO *ITALIAN* The offerings in this small, narrow room will delight diners who've had their fill of Venetian seafood staples—the emphasis here is on well-prepared beef and veal dishes and simple pastas. *Calle dei Assassini, San Marco.* ☎ *041-5286974. Entrees 15€–31€. No credit cards. Open Mon–Sat 12:30–2:30pm, 7:30–11pm. Closed Aug. Vaporetto: Rialto. Map p 93.*

★★★ Vini da Gigio CANNAREGIO *ITALIAN* Wine might get name credit, but the culinary offerings are by no means overlooked: *sarde in saor* (fresh sardines with onions, raisins, and pine nuts), *canestrelli all griglia* (grilled razor clams), and *masorini* (roasted duck) all appear on an innovative menu and are accompanied by a noteworthy selection of wines. *Fondamenta San*

Gondolas glide past canalside diners.

A rustic dining room in the restaurant VinoVino.

Felice. ☎ *041-5285140. Entrees 15€–20€. AE, DC, MC, V. Open Tues–Sun noon–2:30pm, 7:30–10:30pm. Closed part of Aug–Sept and Jan–Feb. Vaporetto: Ca d'Oro. Map p 94.*

★★ **VinoVino** SAN MARCO VENETIAN/SEAFOOD The emphasis in these rustic rooms is on wine by the glass and such homey Venetian favorites as salt cod and fresh sardines. *Ponte delle Veste.* ☎ *041-5237027. Entrees 9€–11€. No credit cards. Open Wed–Mon noon–3:30pm, 7–11pm. Vaporetto: San Marco/Vallaresso. Map p 93.* ●

Salute! Drinking Like a Venetian

Vineyards throughout the Veneto region supply many delightful wines that are perfect accompaniments to seafood and the other fare of which the city is justly proud. Whites, such as the Soaves, tend to be dry, and the reds, Valpolicellas and cabernets dei Friuli among them, fairly light and gentle on the palate. Many Venetians begin the evening with a spritz: a mix of white wine, Campari, Cynar, or another bitter liquor, and sparkling water—most refreshing when deftly blended, disastrously bland when not well concocted. Prosecco, the sparkling white wine from the Veneto, is also often served before a meal, and, though some Venetians might raise an eyebrow at the notion, can continue to be poured through a light repast of seafood. After dessert, out comes the grappa, a headily alcoholic *digestivo* made from fermented skins and seeds left behind when the grapes are pressed for wine.

Nightlife Best Bets

Best **Bellini in the World**
★★★ Harry's Bar, *Calle Vallaresso, San Marco* (p 114)

Best **Place to Blow a Wad on a Cup of Coffee**
★★★ Caffè Florian, *Piazza San Marco* (p 113)

Best **Place to Blow a Wad on a Cup of Coffee If You Can't Get a Table at the Florian**
★★★ Gran Caffé Quadri, *Piazza San Marco* (p 114)

Best **Way to Transport Yourself to a London Pub**
★ Devil's Forest, *Calle Stagneri, San Marco* (p 113)

Best **Pint of Guinness in Town**
★★ Fiddler's Elbow, *Corte dei Pali gia Testori, Cannaregio* (p 113)

Best **Stage in Town: A Boat Moored in the Adjacent Canal**
★★ Paradise Perduto, *Fondamenta della Misericordia, Cannaregio* (p 115)

Best **Place to Bump into Venetian Youth (Literally)**
★ Picolo Mondo, *Calle Contarini Corfù, Dorsoduro* (p 116)

Best **Place to See Young Venetians Peacocking Around in the Wee Hours**
★★ Margaret Duchamp, *Campo Santa Margherita, Dorsoduro* (p 115)

Best **Yuppie-Spotting**
★★ Vitae, *Calle Sant'Antonio, San Marco* (p 115)

Best **Latin Sounds in Town**
★ Round Midnight, *Fondamenta dei Pugni, Dorsoduro* (p 116)

Best **Place to Lose Your Fortune**
★★★ Casino Municipale, *Palazzo Vendramin Calergi, Fondamenta Vendramin, Cannaregio* (p 115)

Best **Selection of Wines by the Glass**
★★ La Caneva, *Calle della Malvasia, Castello* (p 116)

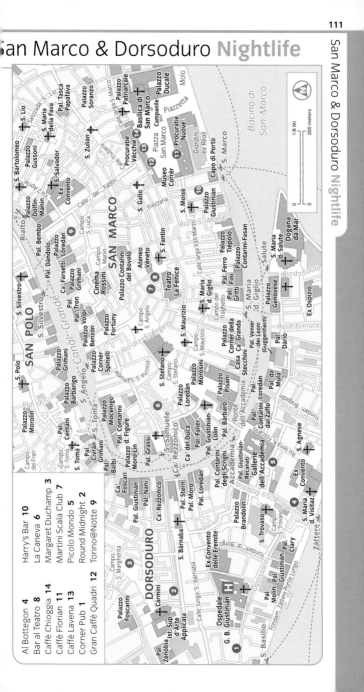

Al Bottegon **4**
Bar al Teatro **8**
Caffè Chioggia **14**
Caffè Florian **11**
Caffè Lavena **13**
Corner Pub **1**
Gran Caffè Quadri **12**

Harry's Bar **10**
La Caneva **6**
Margaret Duchamp **3**
Martini Scala Club **7**
Picolo Mondo **5**
Round Midnight **2**
Torino@Notte **9**

S. Croce, S. Polo & Cannaregio

Alla Mascareta **11**
Bàcaro Jazz **10**
Cantina Do Mori **6**
Casanova Music Cafe **1**
Casino Municipale **3**
Devil's Forest **9**
Fiddler's Elbow **2**
Osteria ai Rusteghi **8**
Osteria del Sacro
e Profano **5**
Paradise Perduto **4**
Vitae **7**

Venice Nightlife A to Z

Cafes & Bars

★★ Bar al Teatro SAN MARCO
Venice's favorite hangout for theatergoers is situated next door to La Fenice and comes alive before and after the opera. *Campo San Fantin.* ☎ *041-5221052. Vaporetto: Sant'Angelo. Map p 111.*

★ Caffè Chioggia SAN MARCO
A Piazza San Marco watering hole that affords ringside views of the moors striking the hours. *Piazza San Marco.* ☎ *041-5285011. Vaporetto: San Marco/Vallaresso. Map p 111.*

★★★ Caffè Florian SAN MARCO
What is probably Venice's most famous cafe—the Quadri, across the square, comes in at a close second—has lost none of its allure since its doors opened in 1720. Goethe and Byron were regulars, and who knows what luminaries might be among the patrons willing to pay so many hard-earned euros to sip an espresso while being serenaded by an orchestra. *Piazza San Marco.* ☎ *041-5205641. www.caffe florian.com. Vaporetto: San Marco/ Vallaresso. Map p 111.*

★★ Caffè Lavena SAN MARCO
A little less flossy than its neighbors on the Piazza, this 250-year-old institution has nonetheless been the favorite of Richard Wagner, Gabriele D'Anunzio, and generations of Venetians. *Piazza San Marco.* ☎ *041-5224070. www.venetia.it/lavena. Vaporetto: San Marco/Vallaresso. Map p 111.*

★ Corner Pub DORSODURO
One of the few funky hangouts in this staid part of town is a quiet retreat during the day, a raucous *boîte de nuit* after dark. *Calle de la Chiesa.* ☎ *340-2581448. Vaporetto: Accademia. Map p 111.*

★ Devil's Forest SAN MARCO
The dart board and London phone box are a hit with Anglophones, but this cozy pub is most popular with locals who linger over beers and games of chess. *Calle Stagneri.* ☎ *041-5200623. Vaporetto: San Marco/Vallaresso. Map p 112.*

★★ Fiddler's Elbow CANNAREGIO Guinness, of course, is on hand and taken seriously at this Irish outpost, as are the soccer matches shown on the large screen out front. *Corte dei Pali gia Testori.* ☎ *041-5239930. Vaporetto: Ca' d'Oro. Map p 112.*

Patrons enjoying cafe society at Caffè Florian, on the Piazza San Marco.

Inside Harry's Bar, a Venetian institution.

★★★ **Gran Caffè Quadri** SAN MARCO   Keeping this long-established watering hole neck and neck with Florian across the Piazza is a similar roster of famous devotees (here including Proust and Stendhal), an equally elegant orchestra, and the same sumptuous views of the domes of the basilica. *Piazza San Marco.* ☎ *041-5222105. www. quadrivenice.com. Vaporetto: San Marco/Vallaresso. Map p 111.*

★★★ **Harry's Bar** SAN MARCO Two reasons to make a stop at this Venetian institution: The Bellini (the sparkling wine/peach juice concoction that's become a brunch-time staple) was invented here, and Hemingway, along with legions of other celebs, drank here. *Calle Vallaresso.* ☎ *041-5285777. www. cipriani.com. Vaporetto: San Marco/ Vallaresso. Map p 111.*

There's Something about Harry's

The most famous bar in Venice—well, maybe the world—opened on the San Marco waterfront in 1931, and people have been talking about the place ever since. Maria Callas and the Aga Kahn were regulars; Harry's was Ernest Hemingway's favorite watering hole; Woody Allen, who loves Venice, pops in from time to time. Some people wouldn't dare darken the noted doorway because Harry's *is* so popular with the rich and famous and the rich and not-so-famous; others go for that very reason. If you do join the legions of travelers who include Harry's on their itinerary, here are some tips. **What to order:** a Bellini, a refreshing concoction of chilled peach juice and Prosecco, and carpaccio, waver-thin slices of beef served with a dollop of mayonnaise and lemon juice. Both were invented at Harry's, and both are named after Venetian painters. **What to bring:** an awful lot of money because Harry's is ridiculously expensive. **What not to bring:** high expectations for friendly service and stunning cuisine because both are underwhelming. **What to wear:** something natty. **What not to wear:** shorts.

★★ Margaret Duchamp

DORSODURO   One of Venice's most popular hangouts keeps the campo animated well into the wee hours. *Campo Santa Margherita.* ☎ *041-286255. Vaporetto: Ca' Rezzonico. Map p 111.*

★★ Vitae SAN MARCO   Chic

surroundings and expertly poured cocktails appeal to a well-heeled younger crowd. *Calle Sant'Antonio.* ☎ *041-5205205. Vaporetto: Rialto. Map p 112.*

Clubs

★★ Bácaro Jazz SAN MARCO

A boisterous cocktail bar doubles as a late-night jazz venue. *Salizzada del Fontego dei Tedeschi, San Marco.* ☎ *041-5285249. Vaporetto: Rialto. Map p 112.*

★ Casanova Music Café

CANNAREGIO   Venetians and visitors of all ages enjoy the city's largest disco, where Friday is salsa night; if you get bored, just pop into the adjoining Internet cafe and check your e-mail. *Lista di Spoagna.* ☎ *041-2750199. Vaporetto: Ferrovia. Map p 112.*

The Casino Municipale.

The Martini Scala Club piano bar.

★★★ Casino Municipale

CANNAREGIO   The surroundings, a 15th-century palace on the Grand Canal, add a sophisticated spin to the proceedings. *Palazzo Vendramin Calergi, Fondamenta Vendramin.* ☎ *041-5297111. Vaporetto: San Marcuola. No admission without jacket for men and passport. Map p 112.*

★★ Martini Scala Club SAN

MARCO   The most elegant piano lounge in town (and perhaps the only one) is the place for a late-night snack accompanied by easy listening. *Campo San Fantin.* ☎ *041-5237027. Vaporetto: Santa Maria del Giglio. Map p 111.*

★★ Paradise Perduto

CANNAREGIO   Jazz, blues, and seafood concoctions draw the crowds. Sit on the terrace and listen to an ensemble playing from a boat moored in the canal alongside—and you'll think you've found paradise. *Fondamenta della Misericordia.* ☎ *041-720581. Vaporetto: Ferrovia. Map p 112.*

The Best Nightlife

The Rialto Bridge at night.

★ **Picolo Mondo** DORSODURO Students from the nearby university get their local disco fix at this small, intimate club, one of very few places in town where you can dance the night away. *Calle Contarini Corfù.* ☎ *041-5200371. Vaporetto: Accademia. Map p 111.*

★ **Round Midnight** DORSODURO Latin sounds prevail on a tiny, cramped dance floor near the university. *Fondamenta dei Pugni.* ☎ *041-5232056. Vaporetto: Accademia. Map p 111.*

★★ **Torino@Notte** SAN MARCO Live jazz some nights and DJ mixes others keep packing in the crowds. *Campo San Luca.* ☎ *041-5223914. Vaporetto: Rialto. Map p 111.*

Osterie (Wine Bars)
★ **Al Bottegon** DORSODURO Take a break from a tour of the nearby Accademia or Peggy Guggenheim Collection and do as the regulars do—step up to the bar, down a glass of Prosecco, and be on your way. *Fondamenta Nani.* ☎ *041-5230034. Vaporetto: Zattere. Map p 111.*

★★ **Alla Mascareta** CASTELLO Wines from vineyards in the surrounding Veneto and Fruili regions are well represented and served by the glass. *Calle Lunga Santa Maria Formosa.* ☎ *041-5230744. Vaporetto: Rialto. Map p 112.*

★★★ **Cantina Do Mori** SAN POLO   In what's said to be the oldest wine bar in town, rows of copper pots hang from the ceiling and wine is poured from huge vats. *Calle Dei Do Mori.* ☎ *041-5225401. Vaporetto: San Silvestro. Map p 112.*

★★ **La Caneva** CASTELLO   Hundreds of wines, many of them from small vineyards whose output you aren't likely to encounter elsewhere, are available by the glass in amiable surroundings. *Calle della Malvasia.* ☎ *041-5212661. Vaporetto: Rialto. Map p 111.*

★★ **Osteria ai Rusteghi** SAN MARCO   A small square is the perfect place to try one of the many wines on offer by the glass, here accompanied by delicious panini. *Campiello del Tentor.* ☎ *041-5232205. Vaporetto: Rialto. Map p 112.*

★ **Osteria del Sacro e Profano** SAN POLO   An excellent selection of wines by the glass and a laid-back atmosphere make this spot popular with a crowd of locals. *Ramo III Parangon.* ☎ *041-5201931. Vaporetto: San Silvestro. Map p 112.* ●

Arts & Entertainment Best Bets

Best **Time to Hide Behind a Mask & Go Wild**
★★★ Carnevale *(p 123)*

Best **Time to Avoid Venice**
★★★ Carnevale *(p 123)*

Best **Place to Watch a Movie under the Stars**
★★ Campo San Polo *(p 122)*

Best **Place to Hear an Organ Recital**
★ Basilica dei Frari *(p 121)*

Best **Time to See Contemporary Art**
★★★ Biennale D'Arte Contemporanea e Architeturra *(p 123)*

Best **Place to Get a Quick Fix of Early Music**
★★ Fondazione Querini Stampalia *(p 121)*

Best **Places to Hear Vivaldi Performed by Musicians in Period Costume**
★★ Scuola Grande di San Teodoro *(p 122)*; and ★★ Chiesa di San Giacomo di Rialto *(p 121)*

Best **Place to Hear a Symphonic Concert**
★★★ Teatro Malibran *(p 122)*

Best **Place to See an Opera**
★★★ La Fenice *(p 122)*

Best **Time to See the Latest International Films**
★★★ Mostra Internazionale d'Arte Cinematografica *(p 122)*

Best **Weekend to Hear Free Music**
★★ Venezia Suona *(p 124)*

Best **Times to Join a Procession and Walk across Water**
★★★ Festa della Madonna della Salute *(p 123)*; and ★★★ Festa del Redentore *(p 124)*

Most **Colorful Time to See the Grand Canal**
★★ Regata Storica *(p 124)*

Best **Place to See Experimental Theater**
★★ Teatro a l'Avogaria *(p 123)*

Most **Mellow Setting for a Concert**
★ Festa di San Pietro *(p 124)*

Getting Tickets

Keep up with cultural happenings around Venice by checking out *Il Gazzettino*, the city's newspaper, and *La Nuova Venezia*, a bimonthly in Italian and English. Tourist offices (p 158) also provide information on concerts and other events. Tickets are usually available at a venue's box office just before a performance. A good one-stop shop for tickets to Venice events is **LaVela**, the ticket agency for the city's transport network. LaVela also markets cultural events; check out the LaVela offices in Calle Fuseri 1810, off the Frezzeria in San Marco (☎ **041-528-7886;** www.actv.it; Mon–Sat 7:30am–7pm), and in Piazzale Roma (☎ **041-272-2249;** www.velaspa.com; daily 7:30am–8pm). Book well in advance for performances that are likely to sell out, such as concerts at the Teatro Malibran and operas at La Fenice.

Santa Croce & San Polo **A&E**

Cannaregio, San Marco & Castello

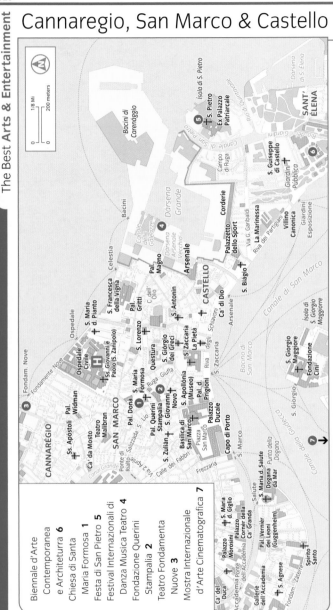

Venice A&E A to Z

Music & Dance

★ Basilica dei Frari SAN POLO
This massive, art-filled church hosts
a fall and spring series of church
music and recitals on the church's
organs. *Campo dei Frari.* ☎ *041-
719308. Vaporetto: San Tomà. Map
p 119.*

**★★ Chiesa di San Giacomo di
Rialto** SAN POLO   The oldest
church in Venice (p 23) is the setting
for concerts by the Ensemble
Antonio Vivaldi, a chamber-music
group whose repertoire ranges from
Mozart to Rossini. *Campo di San
Giacometto.* ☎ *041-4266559. www.
prgroup.it. Tickets 19€. Wed, Fri,
Sun 8:45pm. Tickets on sale at
church from 11am on performance
days. Vaporetto: Rialto. Map p 119.*

**★★ Chiesa di Santa Maria
Formosa** CASTELLO   Collegium
Ducale, a baroque ensemble, per-
forms throughout the year in this
15th-century church. *Campo Santa
Maria Formosa.* ☎ *041-984252.
www.collegiumducale.com. Tickets
20€, 25€. Feb–May Thurs–Sun 9pm;
June, Sept–Jan Thurs, Fri, Sun 9pm.
Box office open from 10:30am on
days of performance. Vaporetto:
Rialto. Map p 120.*

**★★ Fondazione Querini Stam-
palia** CASTELLO   Half-hour recitals
of Renaissance and baroque music
are a nice appetizer for an evening
in Venice. *Campo Santa Maria Formosa.* ☎ *041-2711411. www.querini
stampalia.it. Fri–Sat 5, 8:30pm.
Vaporetto: Rialto. Map p 120.*

**★★ Santa Maria della Visi-
tazione** CANNAREGIO   Antonio
Vivaldi (1678–1741) was a teacher
and choir master at the *ospedale*
(music school) that adjoins this
church, more commonly known as

La Pietà. The oval-shaped apse
beneath ceiling frescoes by Tiepolo is
usually the setting for performances
of the maestro's music by the Centro
di Coordinamento Culturale, but
restoration work has forced a
temporary move to the 15th-century
Palazzo Papafava. *Calle delle Rac-
chette.* ☎ *041-5208767. www.vivaldi.
it. Tickets 25€. Concerts performed
throughout the year on varying schedule. Vaporetto: Ca' d'Oro. Map p 119.*

★★ Scuola Grande dei Carmini
DORSODURO   One of the city's
grandest *scuole* (guild halls) is the
setting for music by Vivaldi and
others, performed by the Venice
Ensemble. *Campo dei Carmini.*
☎ *041-4266559. www.prgroup.it.
Tickets 20€, 25€. Thurs, Sat 8:45pm.
Box office at scuola open 9am–6pm
on days of performance. Vaporetto:
Ca' Rezzonico. Map p 119.*

★ Scuola Grande di San Rocco
SAN POLO   Giovanni Gabrielli and
Claudio Monteverdi are among the
composers associated with this
scuola grande, and the Accademia di
San Rocco often performs their reper-
toire in salons painted by Tintoretto.
Campo San Rocco. ☎ *041-962999.*

Little boy dressed for Carnevale.

www.musicinvenice.com. Ticket prices vary. Vaporetto: San Tomà. Map p 119.

★★ Scuola Grande di San Teodoro

SAN MARCO I Musici Veneziani don period costumes to perform Vivaldi and other baroque masters three evenings a week. Opera arias by Mozart, Rossini, and others are performed two evenings a week. *Salizzada San Teodoro.* ☎ 041-5210294. www.imusici veneziani.com. Tickets 22€–37€. Concert pieces Wed, Fri, Sun 9pm; opera pieces Sat, Tues 9pm. Vaporetto: Rialto. Map p 119.

★★★ Teatro Malibran

CANNAREGIO Built in the 17th century and recently restored, the Malibran is often the venue for concerts by the orchestra of La Fenice, one of Italy's best. The theater also hosts other concerts and dance performances. *Calle dei Milion.* ☎ 899-909090. www.teatrolafenice. it. Vaporetto: Rialto. Map p 119.

Opera

★★★ La Fenice SAN MARCO

The lights are back on in Venice's grand opera house, rebuilt after a fire in 1996. The November-to-June season includes a roster of classic and contemporary operas performed by some of the world's greatest voices. *Campo San Fantin.* ☎ 041-786575. www.teatrolafenice. it. Tickets 35€–200€. Vaporetto: Santa Maria del Giglio. Map p 119.

Cinema

★★ Arena di Campo San Polo

SAN POLO The campo becomes a free outdoor cinema for 6 weeks every summer. Unfortunately, the setting sometimes tops what's on screen, typical Hollywood fare dubbed into Italian. *Campo San Polo.* www.venicebanana.com. Late July to early Sept 9:30pm. Vaporetto: San Tomà. Map p 119.

★ Giorgione Movie d'Essai

CANNAREGIO The repertoire includes foreign-language films; those in English are shown on Tuesdays. *Rio Terà dei Franceschi.* ☎ 041-5226298. Ticket prices vary. Vaporetto: Fondamenta Nuove. Map p 119.

★★★ Mostra Internazionale d'Arte Cinematografica LIDO

Biennale events include one of the world's most prestigious film festivals. Seats are hard to come by; tickets are available from outlets in the city (p 118) and the festival box office in the casino, Lungomare Marconi.

Venice's opera house, La Fenice.

The Rat-King, *a work by Katharina Fritsch, exhibited in the Venice Biennale.*

Palazzo del Cinema, Lungomare Marconi 90, Lido. ☎ *041-5218711. www.labienale.org. Tickets 5€–15€. Vaporetto: Lido. Map p 120.*

Theater

★★ Teatro a l'Avogaria

CANNAREGIO   The theater founded by noted 20th-century director Giovanni Poli continues a tradition of experimental works. *Corte Zappa.* ☎ *041-5206130. Ticket prices vary. Vaporetto: San Basilio. Map p 119.*

★★ Teatro Carlo Goldoni

SAN MARCO   The resident company, Teatro Stabile del Veneto, stages classic Italian drama as well as contemporary works. *Calle Goldoni.* ☎ *041-2402011. www.teatrostabile veneto.it. Mon, Wed, Fri–Sat 8:30 pm; Thurs, Sun 4pm. Ticket prices vary. Vaporetto: Rialto. Map p 119.*

★ Teatro Fondamenta Nuove

CANNAREGIO   The repertoire includes experimental drama, dance, readings, and performance art. *Fondamenta Nuove.* ☎ *041-5224498. Ticket prices vary. Vaporetto: Fondamenta Nuove. Map p 120.*

Festivals & Events

★★★ Biennale D'Arte Contemporanea e Architeturra

CASTELLO   Venice has been staging its prestigious Biennale since 1895, showing the best in contemporary art. Architecture, dance, music, cinema, and theater have been added to the mix over the years. Art and architecture exhibits take over early-20th-century pavilions in the Giardini Pubblici: art in odd years (mid-June to Nov) and architecture in even years (Sept–Oct). *Biennale office: Ca' Giustinian, Calle del Ridotto.* ☎ *041-5218846. www. labiennale.org. Ticket office in Giardini Pubblici. Tickets 15€, 8€ students, 34€ families of up to 2 adults and 2 children. Vaporetto: Giardini. Map p 120.*

★★★ Carnevale

Pre-Lenten celebrations, revived in 1980 to promote winter tourism, draw masked revelers to the city. Highlights include a masked ball. Several masked processions, one in gondolas, snake through the city during the revelries. *10 days before Ash Wednesday. www.carnival ofvenice.com.*

★★★ Festa della Madonna della Salute

DORSODURO   Like Il Redentore (below), the Chiesa della Madonna della Salute (see p 11, bullet ❶) was built as an offering for relief from a plague epidemic, this one in 1630. On November 21, Venetians give thanks by making the pilgrimage across the Grand Canal on a specially built pontoon bridge to light candles in the church.

Vaporetto: San Marco/Vallaresso or Salute. Map p 119.

★★★ Festa del Redentore

GIUDECCA   The church of Il Redentore (see p 46, bullet ❶) was begun in 1576 as an offering of thanks to the Redeemer for delivering Venice from a plague epidemic. Ever since, the city has set aside the third weekend in July as the time to make a pilgrimage to the church and offer thanks anew. Once a colorful bridge of boats facilitated the trip across the Guidecca canal; these days the Italian army builds a temporary pontoon bridge. On Saturday evening, fireworks light the sky. *Vaporetto: Zattere or Redentore. Map p 119.*

★ Festa di San Pietro   CASTELLO

In the last week of June, the waterside lawns beneath the leaning campanile of the Chiesa di San Pietro in Castello are filled with revelers celebrating the saint's feast and enjoying a series of concerts. *Vaporetto: San Pietro. Map p 120.*

★★ Festival Internazionali di Danza Musica Teatro   CASTELLO

The International Festival of Dance, Music, and Theater debuts in newly renovated theaters in the Arsenale, the Fenice, and other venues. The music and theater festivals take place in late September and early October; the dance festival in June. *Biennale office: Ca' Giustinian, Calle del Ridotto.* ☎ *041-5218846. www. labiennale.org. Tickets: dance & music*

Dog dressed up for Carnevale.

13€–25€; theater 8€–10€ students. Vaporetto: Arsenale. Map p 120.

★★ Regata Storica

The Grand Canal becomes a stage for processions and boat races on the first Sunday in September. *Map p 119.*

★★ Teatro in Campo   DORSO-

DURO   Plays, operas, and dance performances are staged in Campo Pisani, in the garden of the Peggy Guggenheim Collection, the cloisters of San Giobbe, and other evocative locales around the city and on the islands. Organized by Pantakin da Venezia, a cultural organization. ☎ *041-5221740. Tickets from 13€. Vaporetto: Salute. Map p 119.*

★★ Venezia Suona

Musicians take over many *campi* around the city for a day of free concerts, from baroque to hard rock. *Sun closest to June 21.* ☎ *041-2750049. www. veneziasuona.it.* ●

The colorful procession of boats at the Regata Storica.

9 The Best Lodging

Lodging Best Bets

Most Hip
★★★ Ca' Pisani $$$. *Rio Terrà Antonio Foscarini, Dorsoduro (see p 134)*

Best Place to Hang Out by the Pool
★★★ Cipriani $$$$. *Giudecca 10 (see p 135)*

Best Lobby in Venice
★★★ Danieli $$$$. *Riva Degli Schiavoni, Castello (see p 136)*

Best Place to be Pampered in Luxury
★★★ Gritti Palace $$$$. *Campo Santa Maria del Giglio, San Marco (see p 136)*

Best Place to Stay in Style without Breaking the Bank
★★★ Hotel Al Piave. *Ruga Giuffa, Castello (see p 137)*

Classiest Place Near the Train Station
★★ Hotel Bellini. *Lista di Spagna, Cannaregio (see p 138)*

Best Place to Be Decadent
★★★ Hotel des Bains $$$$. *Lungomare Marconi 17, Lido (see p 138)*

Best Palace Hotel for the Money
★★★ La Residenza $–$$. *Campo Bandiera e Moro, Castello (see p 141)*

Best Place to Get Away from It All
★★★ Locanda Cipriani $$$–$$$$. *Piazza Santa Fosca 29, Torcello (see p 141)*

Best Hotel Garden
★★★ Pensione Accademia/Villa Maravege $$–$$$. *Fondamenta Bollani, Dorsoduro (see p 143)*

Best Place to Savor the Rialto Markets
★★ Pensione Guerrato $. *Calle Drio la Scimia, San Polo (see p 144)*

Best Old-Fashioned Pensione Experience
★★★ Pensione Seguso $$. *Fondamenta Zattere ai Geuati, Dorsoduro (see p 144)*

Best Bargain View of the Grand Canal
★★★ Hotel Galleria $–$$. *Rio Terrà Antonio Foscarini (see p 139)*

San Marco & Castello **Lodging**

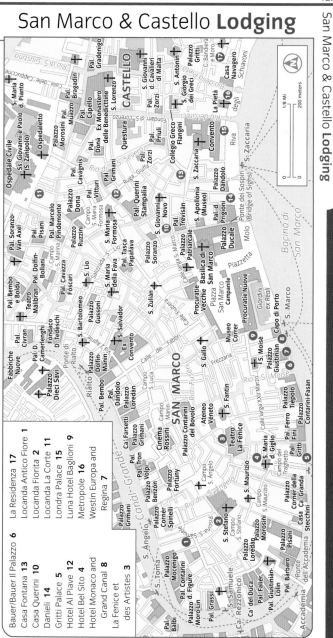

Bauer/Bauer Il Palazzo **6**
Casa Fontana **13**
Casa Querini **10**
Danieli **14**
Gritti Palace **5**
Hotel Al Piave **12**
Hotel Bel Sito **4**
Hotel Monaco and
   Grand Canal **8**
La Fenice et
   des Artistes **3**
La Residenza **17**
Locanda Antico Fiore **1**
Locanda Fiorita **2**
Locanda La Corte **11**
Londra Palace **15**
Luna Hotel Baglioni **9**
Metropole **16**
Westin Europa and
   Regina **7**

Cannaregio **Lodging**

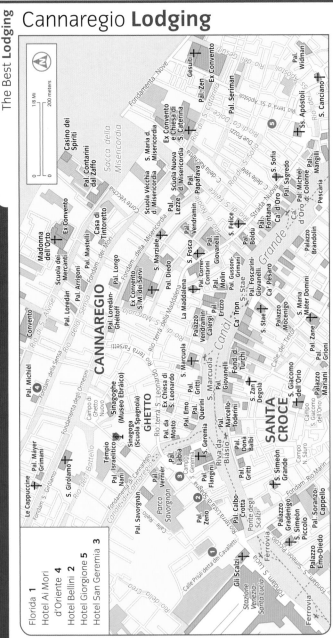

Dorsoduro & Giudecca **Lodging**

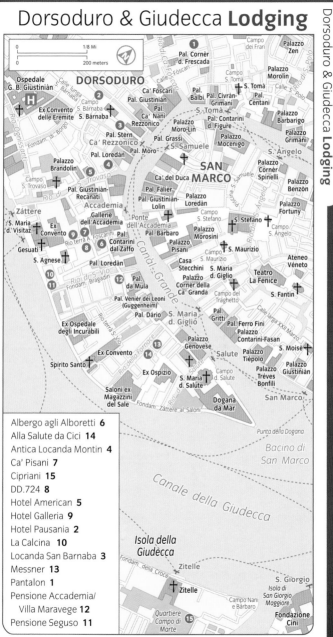

Albergo agli Alboretti **6**
Alla Salute da Cici **14**
Antica Locanda Montin **4**
Ca' Pisani **7**
Cipriani **15**
DD.724 **8**
Hotel American **5**
Hotel Galleria **9**
Hotel Pausania **2**
La Calcina **10**
Locanda San Barnaba **3**
Messner **13**
Pantalon **1**
Pensione Accademia/
    Villa Maravege **12**
Pensione Seguso **11**

The Lido & Torcello **Lodging**

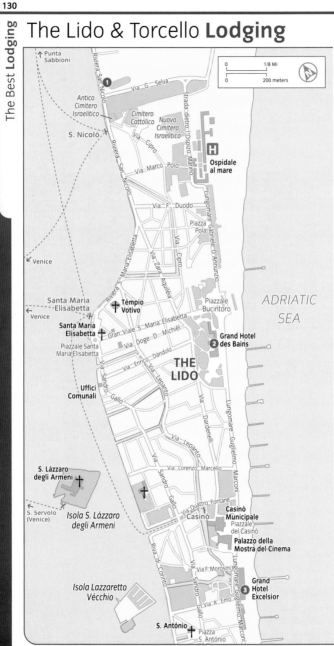

- Punta Sabbioni
- Via G. Selva
- Strada dietro l'Ospizio Marino
- **1**
- Antico Cimitero Israelitico
- Cimitero Cattólico
- Nuovo Cimitero Israelitico
- S. Nicolò
- Via Cipro
- Riviera San Nicolò
- Via Marco Polo
- **H** Ospidale al mare
- Via F. Duodo
- Lungomare Gabriele D'Annunzio
- Piazza Pola
- Venice
- Via Zara
- Via Cipro
- Riviera S. Maria Elisabetta
- Santa Maria Elisabetta
- Venice
- † Témpio Votivo
- Aquiléia
- Piazzale Bucintoro
- **ADRIATIC SEA**
- Santa Maria Elisabetta †
- Gran Viale S. Maria Elisabetta
- Via Doge D. Michiel
- **Grand Hotel 2 des Bains**
- Piazzale Santa Maria Elisabetta
- Via Enrico Dándolo
- Via Sandro Gallo
- **THE LIDO**
- Uffici Comunali
- Via Lepanto
- Via Darderelli
- Lungomare Guglielmo Marconi
- S. Lázzaro degli Armeni †
- Via Sandro Gallo
- Via Lorenzo Marcello
- S. Servolo (Venice)
- Isola S. Lázzaro degli Armeni
- †
- Via Quattro Fontane
- Casinó
- **Casinò Municipale**
- Piazzale del Casinó
- **Palazzo della Mostra del Cinema**
- Isola Lazzaretto Vécchio
- Riva di Corinto
- Via F. Morosini
- **Grand 3 Hotel Excelsior**
- Via A. Emo
- Via Sandro Gallo
- Lungomare Guglielmo Marconi
- S. António †
- Piazza S. António

0 | 1/8 Mi
0 | 200 meters

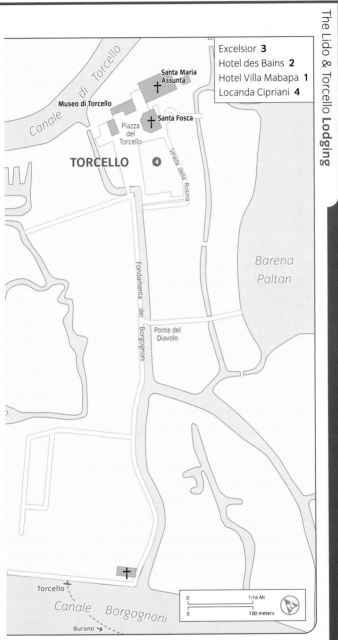

Excelsior **3**
Hotel des Bains **2**
Hotel Villa Mabapa **1**
Locanda Cipriani **4**

Santa Maria
Assunta

Museo di Torcello

Canale di Torcello

Santa Fosca

Piazza
del
Torcello

TORCELLO **4**

Strada della Rosina

Barena
Paltan

Fondamenta dei Borognoni

Ponte del
Diavolo

Torcello

Canale Borgognoni

Burano

0   1/16 Mi
0   100 meters

San Polo & Santa Croce **Lodging**

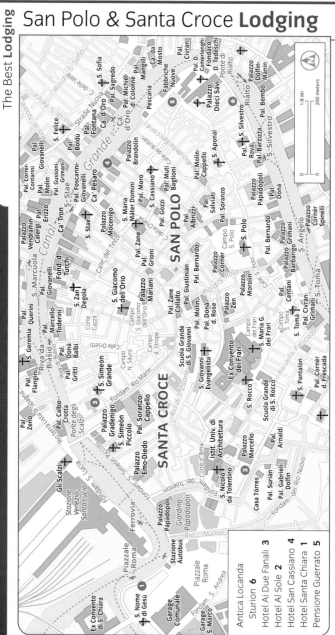

Venice Hotels A to Z

A vintage concierge lamp in a Venice hotel.

★ **Albergo agli Alboretti** NEAR THE ACCADEMIA   The plain, modern furnishings are not much more than serviceable and accommodations can be tight, but the location in a quiet residential neighborhood near the Accademia and the Guggenheim and the lovely rear garden may well atone for these lapses. *Rio Terrà Antonio*

Foscarini, Dorsoduro. ☎ *041-5230058. www.aglialboretti.com. 14 units. Doubles 150€–180€. AE, MC, V. Vaporetto: Accademia. Map p 129.*

★★ **Alla Salute da Cici** NEAR SALUTE   A 16th-century palazzo in the backwaters of the Dorsoduro offers high-ceiling guest rooms with Grand Canal or garden views, while quarters in a modern annex trade character for such modern conveniences as air-conditioning and shiny new bathrooms. *Fondamenta Ca' Balà, Dorsoduro.* ☎ *041-5235404. www.hotelsalute.com. 58 units. Doubles 120€–140€. AE, MC, V. Vaporetto: Salute. Map p 129.*

★ **Antica Locanda Montin** NEAR THE ACCADEMIA   A pretty garden, a homey, low-key atmosphere, and views of a small canal— along with bargain prices for the location—compensate for the worn decor and fairly spartan amenities. *Fondamenta Eremite, Dorsoduro.* ☎ *041-5227151. www.locanda montin.com. 12 units. Doubles 85€–140€. AE, MC, V. Vaporetto: Accademia. Map p 129.*

★★ **Antica Locanda Sturion** RIALTO   Two large rooms overlooking the Grand Canal are the top

A Price for All Seasons

Accommodations in Venice are never inexpensive, but at some times of the year they are especially expensive. June through August, Christmas and New Year's holidays, and Carnivale are unofficially high season, when rates can double or even triple those of other times of the year. Many hotels consider May and September to October to be middle season, and classify the rest of the year as low season. Prices fluctuate wildly, though—if a hotel has vacancies, no matter what the season, prices might come down.

choices in this 13th-century inn that's just steps from the Rialto bridge, but all the accommodations are loaded with character and the common areas enjoy the knockout view, too. Some of the rooms nicely accommodate families, and the kids come in handy when it's time to carry bags up and down the many flights of stairs. *Calle del Sturion, San Polo.* ☎ *041-5236243. www. locandasturion.com. 11 units. Doubles 120€–250€. AE, MC, V. Vaporetto: San Silvestro. Map p 132.*

★★ Bauer/Bauer Il Palazzo

NEAR PIAZZA SAN MARCO   Choose between an 18th-century palazzo on the Grand Canal and a 1950s addition. Antiques-filled, high-ceilinged palazzo rooms are the swankiest, no surprise, but there's nothing shoddy about the newer rooms, which look like luxurious Hollywood movie sets. Guests in all enjoy a stunning rooftop terrace and a chance to slip into a gondola from the hotel dock. *Campo San Moisè, San Marco.* ☎ *041-5207022. www.bauervenezia. it. 190 units. Doubles 300€–550€. MC, V. Vaporetto: San Marco/ Vallaresso. Map p 127.*

★★★ Ca' Pisani

NEAR THE ACCADEMIA   A 16th-century palazzo, art moderne furnishings, and wonderful paintings by the Italian futurist Fortunato Depero blend

Typically colorful Venice hotel keys.

harmoniously in this high-design, high-chic hostelry. But some traditional elements, such as the quiet neighborhood and proximity to the Accademia, are also part of the appeal. *Rio Terrà Antonio Foscarini, 979a, Dorsoduro.* ☎ *041-2401411. www.capisanihotel.it. 29 units. Doubles 238€–276€. MC, V. Vaporetto: Accademia. Map p 129.*

★★ Casa Fontana

NEAR PIAZZA SAN MARCO   The Stainer family has been welcoming guests to their convent-turned-hotel for 40 years, providing a snug retreat from the hustle and bustle of nearby San

A Room with a View?

That's not always a blessing in Venice. First of all, a view of any water—especially of the Grand Canal—usually pushes the price up considerably. Second, a room with a view of a waterway can be noisy because canals are the city's streets—and the noise of a boat collecting garbage at 4am is no more romantic than that of a truck doing the same chore in the street. Not to say that some Venetian views aren't utterly charming—just be sure to ask what you're going to be paying for the privilege of seeing before you book.

Location, Location, Location

Getting lost in Venice can be a pleasure, but not when you're dragging luggage over bridges and up and down stairs as you look for your hotel. When booking, find out exactly *where* your hotel is, *where* the nearest vaporetto stop is, and the easiest way to get from the stop to the hotel. Many hotels print maps on their websites, but if it's not detailed, don't bother—buy yourself a good map instead and locate your hotel and arrival route on that.

Marco. The reassuringly old-fashioned rooms have updated bathrooms and overlook Campo San Provolo or Campo San Zaccaria and its stunning church; two rooms have private terraces. *Campo San Provolo, Castello.* ☎ *041-5220579. www. hotelfontana.com. 16 units. Doubles 80€–170€. AE, MC, V. Vaporetto: San Zaccaria. Map p 127.*

★ **Casa Querini** NEAR PIAZZA SAN MARCO This old palazzo in a quiet square seems miles from San Marco, when it's actually just a few minutes away. A small terrace on the campo is a nice place to watch the neighborhood comings and goings, and the rooms upstairs are unusually spacious and pleasantly decorated in the ubiquitous hotel

"Venetian antique" style. *Campo San Giovanni Novo, Castello.* ☎ *041-2411294. www.locandaquerini.com. 11 units. Doubles 93€–197€. AE, MC, V. Vaporetto: San Zaccaria. Map p 127.*

★★★ **Cipriani** GIUDECCA A getaway just minutes from San Marco (and reached by private launch) pampers guests with luxurious accommodations in a cluster of centuries-old buildings and with such amenities as a gorgeous swimming pool, a spa, tennis courts, lush gardens, and waterside bars and restaurants. *Giudecca 10.* ☎ *041-5207744. www.hotelcipriani.it. 96 units. Doubles 625€–815€. MC, V. Closed Nov–Mar. Vaporetto: Zitelle. Map p 129.*

Cipriani hotel waterside restaurant.

The Danieli hotel's extravagant lobby.

★★★ **Danieli** SAN MARCO   A marble-clad entrance to a 13th-century doge's palace wins the prize for the best lobby in Venice, and the rooms upstairs in what is one of the finest hotels anywhere are no less opulent—even those in the "new" adjoining 19th- and 20th-century wings. *Riva Degli Schiavoni, Castello.* ☎ *041-5226480. www.starwood. com/luxury. 235 units. Doubles 410€– 650€. AE, D, MC, V. Vaporetto: San Zaccaria. Map p 127.*

★★★ **DD.724** NEAR THE ACCADE-MIA & GUGGENHEIM   A contemporary, sophisticated style pervades this chic little inn, tucked away near the museums, Salute, and other prime Dorsoduro sights. Some rooms and the lounge overlook a small garden. *Rio Terrà Antonio Foscarini, Dorsoduro.* ☎ *041-2770262. www.dd724.it. 8 units. Doubles 200€–330€. MC, V. Vaporetto: Accademia. Map p 129.*

★★★ **Excelsior** LIDO   This exotic palace by the sea, one of Europe's grandest hotels, has all the resort amenities—private beach, swimming pool, golf privileges, tennis—you could ever want or need. But you may choose never to leave the sumptuous, Moorish-themed rooms, many with sitting alcoves and all with a view of the sea, lagoon, or lush gardens. *Lungomare Guglielmo Marconi*

41, Lido. ☎ *041-5260201. www. starwood.com/westin. 195 units. Doubles 400€–700€. AE, DC, MC, V. Closed Nov–Mar. Vaporetto: Terrazza, Tropicana. Map p 131.*

★ **Florida** NEAR THE TRAIN STA-TION   Even if you don't have a train to catch, these sparkling-clean and comfortable, faux-antique-furnished rooms are worth considering— they're a real bargain, and offer air-conditioning and other amenities not usually found in this price range. *Calle Priuli dei Cavaletti, Cannaregio.* ☎ *041-715253. www.hotel-florida.com. 24 units. Doubles 75€–90€. AE, MC, V. Vaporetto: Ferrovia. Map p 128.*

⓮ ★★★ **Gritti Palace** NEAR PIAZZA SAN MARCO   Doge Andrea Gritti built this palazzo in 1525, and the sheen of luxury hasn't faded since—making the Gritti a top choice for guests who expect to be pampered amid all the trappings of grandeur. Immense rooms and suites groan under the weight of swags, ornate mirrors, and Venetian antiques, and many overlook the Grand Canal. *Campo Santa Maria del Giglio, San Marco.* ☎ *041-794611. www.starwood.com/luxury. 91 units. Doubles 500€–850€. AE, DC, MC, V. Vaporetto: San Zaccaria. Map p 127.*

★★★ Hotel Ai Due Fanali

SANTA CROCE A 14th-cenutry building that was once part of the nearby church of San Simeone Profeta Campo is still graced with enough frescoes, paneling, and antiques (the check-in desk is an old altar) to lend a wonderfully quirky old-world air to the place. Wooden beams, painted headboards, terra-cotta tiles, and an occasional glimpse of the Grand Canal enliven the charming guest rooms. The establishment also rents four apartments near San Marco. *San Simeone Profeta, Santa Croce.* ☎ *041-718490. www.aiduefanali.com. 16 units. Doubles 95€–210€. AE, MC, V. Vaporetto: Ferrovia. Map p 132.*

★★★ Hotel Ai Mori d'Oriente

NEAR THE GHETTO A house once occupied by Turkish traders still exudes an exotic air, with Turkish carpets and furnishings setting the guest rooms apart from the ordinary. *Fondamenta della Sensa, Cannaregio.* ☎ *041-711001. www. hotelaimoridoriente.it. 55 units. Doubles 150€–410€. MC, V. Vaporetto: Orto. Map p 128.*

★★★ Hotel Al Piave NEAR RIVA

DEGLI SCHIAVONI Who says you must pay high prices for high style? Tastefully appointed rooms combine luxurious fabrics and furnishings with wooden beams, polished tile floors, and other architectural features to provide the sort of comfortable lodgings in which you'll actually want to spend time. *Ruga Giuffa, Castello.* ☎ *041-5285174. www. hotelpiave.com. 13 units. Doubles 130€–190€. AE, MC, V. Vaporetto: San Zaccaria. Map p 127.*

★★ Hotel Al Sole NEAR CAMPO

SANTA MARGHERITA Palazzi-turned-hotels are hardly a rarity in Venice, but this one stands out with its lovely location on a canal and close to the Frari, San Rocco, and the lively Campo Santa Margherita. Guest rooms are cozily adorned with the occasional beamed ceiling and antique furnishings, and most have pleasant views onto the palace's own garden or the neighboring rooftops. *Fondamenta Minotto, Santa Croce.* ☎ *041-2440328. www.alsolehotels. com. 62 units. Doubles 120€–290€. AE, DC, MC, V. Vaporetto: Piazzale Roma. Map p 132.*

A marbled bar in the Gritti Palace.

A charming room, with balcony, in the Hotel American.

★★★ **Hotel American** NEAR THE ACCADEMIA Large rooms furnished in antique Venetian style and a lovely terrace provide just the right atmosphere for a retreat in this quiet corner of the Dorsoduro neighborhood—in some rooms, flower-filled balconies overlooking a small canal add an extra dose of charm. *Fondamenta Bragadin, Dorsoduro.* ☎ *041-5204733. www.hotel american.com. 30 units. Doubles 180€–250€. AE, MC, V. Vaporetto: Accademia. Map p 129.*

The tree-shaded pool at the Hotel des Bains.

★★ **Hotel Bellini** NEAR THE TRAIN STATION The location is a real asset for early morning departures or short stays when the idea of lugging baggage on and off boats doesn't seem worth the effort. Acres of marble and plush upholstery shield guests from the fray of the busy neighborhood outside, and some rooms have views of the Grand Canal. *Lista di Spagna, Cannaregio.* ☎ *041-5242488. www.bellini.boscolo hotels.com. 97 units. Doubles 159€– 409€. AE, D, MC, V. Vaporetto: Ferrovia. Map p 128.*

★★★ **Hotel Bel Sito** BETWEEN PIAZZA SAN MARCO & THE ACCADEMIA BRIDGE There's an air of quiet elegance to this small hotel, in which reproduction antiques and tasteful fabrics make the cozy rooms unusually pleasant and restful. The neighborhood is quiet but within an easy walk of both the Accademia and San Marco. *Campo Santa Maria del Giglio, San Marco.* ☎ *041-5223365. 34 units. Doubles 130€–175€. AE, MC, V. Vaporetto: Giglio. Map p 127.*

★★★ **Hotel des Bains** LIDO The beach, pools, tennis courts, and other amenities provide all you'll need for a complete vacation at this Art Nouveau resort hotel where

Thomas Mann wrote and set *Death in Venice*. The place still sets the gold standard for an old-world pampered retreat. The large rooms and lounges stylishly retain their century-old glamour, and there's just enough of a whiff of decadence to satisfy fans of the novel and film. *Lungomare Marconi 17, Lido.* ☎ *041-5265921. www.starwood. com. 191 units. Doubles 250€–450€. AE, D,MC, V. Closed Nov–Mar. Vaporetto: Lido. Map p 131.*

★★★ **Hotel Galleria** NEAR THE ACCADEMIA   One of the biggest bargains in Venice is this pleasant little *pensione* right on the Grand Canal. Rooms have been pleasantly redone in traditional Venetian style, but all you'll really care about is the captivating waterway beneath your window. *Rio Terrà Antonio Foscarini, Dorsoduro.* ☎ *041-5232489. www. hotelgalleria.it. 34 units. Doubles 105€–155€. AE, MC, V. Vaporetto: Accademia. Map p 129.*

The Hotel des Bains.

★★ **Hotel Giorgione** NEAR RIALTO   An off-the-beaten-track location and charming courtyard assure a sense of calm, as do the handsome rooms and suites with their rich fabrics, painted furniture, and gleaming bathrooms. Most of the junior suites are spread out over two floors, assuring a bit of home-like privacy for families. *Campo dei Santi Apostoli, Cannaregio.* ☎ *041-5225810. www.hotelgiorgione.com. 76 units. Doubles 150€–310€. AE, MC, V. Vaporetto: Ca d'Oro. Map p 128.*

★★★ **Hotel Monaco and Grand Canal** NEAR PIAZZA SAN MARCO   Location is no small part of the appeal of this 17th-century palazzo-turned-grand-hotel, just steps from the Piazza and right on the Grand Canal, which laps against the delightful terrace. The best of the comfortably luxurious, recently redecorated rooms overlook the canal. *San Marco 1325, San Marco.* ☎ *041-5200211. www. summithotels.com. 44 units. Doubles 190€–420€. AE, D, MC, V. Vaporetto: San Marco/Vallaresso. Map p 127.*

★★ **Hotel Pausania** NEAR CAMPO SAN BARNABA   The entrance to this 14th-century palazzo is through a stunning courtyard with a well and an exterior stone staircase. Guest rooms are a bit less atmospheric, but have benefited from a thorough renovation and are comfortably if unimaginatively furnished in traditional style; each room has its own tidy little bathroom. *Fondamenta Gerardini, Dorsoduro.* ☎ *041-5222083. www.veniceby.com/pausania. 24 units. Doubles 70€–250€. AE, D, MC, V. Vaporetto: Ca' Rezzonico. Map p 129.*

Room at the Hotel San Cassiano.

★★ Hotel San Cassiano ON THE
GRAND CANAL A small palazzo on the Grand Canal, home to 19th-century painter Giacomo Favretto and other notable Venetians, now houses simply furnished but delightful rooms, some facing the famous waterway—the colorful scene is also enjoyed from the waterside terrace. *Calle della Rosa, Santa Croce.* ☎ *041-5241768. www.san cassiano.it. 35 units. Doubles 120€–360€. MC, V. Vaporetto: San Stae. Map p 132.*

★★★ Hotel San Geremia
CANNAREGIO The off-the-beaten-track location on a lovely campo is one of many attributes of this pleasant little hotel. Others are the bright rooms sponge-painted in soothing earth tones and nicely done up with contemporary furnishings—and offered at an extremely reasonable price. Ask for a room facing the campo, or, if you don't mind climbing stairs, one of the top-floor units with terraces. *Campo San Geremia, Cannaregio.* ☎ *041-716245. www.sangeremia.com. 20 units. Doubles 90€–150€. AE, DC, MC, V. Vaporetto: Ferrovia. Map p 128.*

★★ Hotel Santa Chiara NEAR
PIAZZALE ROMA The handy proximity of the car parks and bus stops of Piazzale Roma doesn't suggest a pleasant getaway, but that's what this bright and welcoming hotel is. Many of the appealing rooms face the Grand Canal; some have private terraces. *Fondamenta Santa Chiara, Santa Croce.* ☎ *041-5222083. www. hotelsantachiara.com. 28 units. Doubles 220€. AE, MC, V. Vaporetto: Piazzale Roma. Map p 132.*

★★ Hotel Villa Mabapa LIDO
An Art Nouveau villa and two adjoining houses, just steps from the beach and set in a large, leafy garden, provide a nice way to enjoy the Lido without having to pay the higher cost of one of the posher resorts. All of the large guest rooms are different, and many retain 1930s-style furnishings. *Riviera San Nicolò, Lido.* ☎ *041-5260590. www.mabapa.it. 34 units. Doubles 192€–236€. AE, MC, V. Vaporetto: Lido. Map p 131.*

★★★ La Calcina ON THE ZATTERE
British essayist John Ruskin wrote part of the *Stones of Venice* here, and the years have been kind to this pleasantly old-fashioned hotel overlooking the Giudecca Canal. Recent

La Calcina hotel.

The 15th-century pensione La Residenza.

renovations have buffed up the parquet floors and put a shine on the comfortable old furniture. The waterside terrace is a fine place to lounge. *Fondamenta Zattere ai Geuati, Dorsoduro.* ☎ *041-5206466. www.lacalcina.com. 29 units. Doubles 99€–186€. MC, V. Vaporetto: Zattere or Accademia. Map p 129.*

★★ **La Fenice et des Artistes** NEAR PIAZZA SAN MARCO   This old-fashioned favorite with opera buffs and stars from the nearby Fenice theater encompasses two 19th-century palaces, and offers homey, comfortable rooms (all with new bathrooms), rather grand public areas, and even a pretty little garden. *Campiello della Fenice, San Marco.* ☎ *041-5232333. www.fenicehotels.it. 70 units. Doubles 135€–270€. AE, D, MC, V. Vaporetto: Santa Maria del Giglio. Map p 127.*

★★★ **La Residenza** NEAR RIVA DEGLI SCHIAVONI   Top prize for palatial and atmospheric lodgings at a good price goes to this old-fashioned pensione that occupies the 15th-century Palazzo Gritti Badoer. The lobby is a period piece of polished wood, chandeliers, and oil paintings, while the large high-ceiling guest rooms have all been beautifully refurbished with wood flooring and reproduction antiques that do justice to the lovely surroundings. *Campo Bandiera e Moro, Castello.* ☎ *041-5285315. www.venicelaresidenza.com. 14 units. Doubles: 80€–160€. AE, MC, V. Vaporetto: Arsenale. Map p 127.*

★★ **Locanda Antico Fiore** SAN MARCO   These large, tasteful, but no-frills lodgings are a relative bargain, and the location—in a quiet corner of town just steps from the Grand Canal and Accademia bridge—is superb. *Corte Lucatello, San Marco.* ☎ *041-5227941. www.anticofiore.com. 33 units. Doubles 125€–145€. MC, V. Vaporetto: San Samuele. Map p 127.*

★★★ **Locanda Cipriani** TORCELLO A much-touted celebrity retreat lives up to its rep as a haven of casual elegance. Guests are cosseted by such homey amenities as plush armchairs and excellent beds, a lovely garden, and a noted restaurant (see p 104). Best of all, guests have the enchanting island almost to themselves when the day-trippers leave. *Piazza Santa*

Locanda Cipriani, on the island of Torcello.

The courtyard at the Locanda La Corte.

Fosca 29, Torcello. ☎ 041-730150. www.locandacipriani.com. 6 units. Doubles 240€–340€. AE, D, MC, V. Vaporetto: Torcello. Map p 131.

★★ **Locanda Fiorita** NEAR PIZZA SAN MARCO   A recent spruce-up has left this little palazzo more charming than ever. The shiny bathrooms and handsome, 18th-century Venetian-style furnishings and fabrics are new, but old favorites like the wisteria-shaded terrace overlooking the campiello remain. Some rooms are situated in a nearby annex, Ca' Morosini, but opt for one in the palazzo. Campiello Nuovo, San Marco. ☎ 041-5234754. www. locandafiorita.com. 16 units. Doubles 110€–130€. AE, MC, V. Vaporetto: San Samuele. Map p 127.

★★★ **Locanda La Corte** CASTELLO   The eponymous courtyard, most welcome after a summer's day of exploring, along with exposed beams, polished floors, and plenty of other 16th-century embellishments, make this small palazzo a cozy and stylish retreat in a pretty backwater of the city. Calle Bressana, Castello (near Campo San Giovanni e Paolo). ☎ 041-2411300. www.locandala corte.it. 16 units. Doubles 160€–185€. AE, MC, V. Vaporetto: Fondamenta Nove. Map p 127.

★★★ **Londra Palace** RIVA DEGLI SCHIAVONI   This 19th-century neo-Gothic palace laden with oil paintings and antiques inspired Tchaikovsky to write his fourth symphony—but it's quite alright if you're moved to do nothing more than enjoy the water views from one of the sumptuous guest rooms or the airy roof terrace. Do Leoni, one of Venice's best restaurants, is on the premises. Riva degli Schiavoni, Castello. ☎ 041-5200533. www.hotel ondra.it. 53 units. Doubles 275€–585€. AE, DC, MC, V. Vaporetto: San Zaccaria. Map p 127.

★★★ **Locanda San Barnaba** DORSODURO   The pretty garden and sunny roof terrace make it difficult to spend too much time indoors, but the guest rooms are delightful—crisscrossed by ancient timbers and nicely done up with Turkish carpets, painted bureaus, plump armchairs, and other comfy trappings. A two-level junior suite is especially handy for travelers with kids in tow. Calle del Traghetto, Dorsoduro. ☎ 041-2411233. www. locanda-sanbarnaba.com. 13 units. Doubles 130€–160€. AE, MC, V. Vaporetto: Ca' Rezzonico. Map p 129.

★★★ **Luna Hotel Baglioni** NEAR PIAZZA SAN MARCO   Said to date from the 12th century, the oldest hotel in Venice is also one of the best located, with the Bacino San Marco lapping its walls and Piazza San Marco just around the corner. Only a few of the rooms, the most expensive ones, of course, enjoy water views, but all are posh and stylishly appointed with marble bathrooms and modern conveniences. *Calle Larga dell'Ascensione, San Marco.* ☎ *041-5289840. www.baglioni.com. 109 units. Doubles 250€–450€. AE, D, MC, V. Vaporetto: San Marco/ Vallaresso. Map p 127.*

★★ **Messner** NEAR SALUTE Guest rooms are spread throughout three nearby buildings, and while the decor is fairly standard hotel modern throughout, those in the 14th-century palazzo enjoy high ceilings, tall windows, and other old-world touches. Some rooms overlook a delightful garden and others a canal, and the glorious waterfront around Salute is just steps away. *Fondamenta Ca' Balà, Dorsoduro.* ☎ *041-5227443. www. hotelmessner.it. 33 units. Doubles 115€–160€. AE, MC, V. Vaporetto: Salute. Map p 129.*

★★ **Metropole** RIVA DEGLI SCHIAVONI Venice's own master of Baroque music, Antonio Vivaldi,

once lived in this palazzo, and the maestro might still feel right at home amid the bric-a-brac and swirls of fabric. Rooms vary widely in decor (a few are almost contemporary in feel) and in outlook, but most have a view—be it of the Bacino San Marco, a side canal, or the lovely rear garden. *Riva degli Schiavoni, Castello.* ☎ *041-5205044. www.hotelmetropole.com. 72 units. Doubles 150€–600€. AE, MC, V. Vaporetto: San Zaccaria. Map p 127.*

★ **Pantalon** NEAR THE UNIVERSITY The basic rooms decorated in plain, modern furnishings are perfectly comfortable and the service is commendable, but this hotel's best assets are the sunny roof terrace and the lively neighborhood scene. *Crosera San Pantalon, Dorsoduro.* ☎ *041-718683. www.hotelpantalon. com. 24 units. Doubles 90€–140€. AE, MC, V. Vaporetto: San Tomà. Map p 129.*

★★★ **Pensione Accademia/ Villa Maravege** NEAR THE ACCADEMIA A patrician villa that served as the Russian consulate until the 1930s still exudes the air of a private home, with comfortable lounges, antiques-filled rooms, and two large gardens. If the place looks

The facade of the Pensione Accademia/Villa Maravege.

The Pensione Seguso has views of the Giudecca canal.

familiar, there's good reason: It's the charming spot where Katherine Hepburn's character stayed in the David Lean movie *Summertime*. *Fondamenta Bollani, Dorsoduro.* ☎ *041-5210188. www.pensione accademia.it. 27 units. Doubles 130€–275€. AE, MC, V. Vaporetto: Accademia. Map p 129.*

★★ **Pensione Guerrato** RIALTO Staying smack in the middle of the Rialto market area can be a heady but tiring experience, and these old-fashioned, high-ceilinged rooms in a former convent, furnished with an eclectic and charming mix of antiques, provide a welcome retreat. A choice few have partial views of

the Grand Canal. *Calle Drio la Scimia, San Polo.* ☎ *041-5285927. http:// web.tiscali.it/pensioneguerrato. 14 units. Doubles 95€–125€. AE, MC, V. Vaporetto: Rialto. Map p 136.*

★★★ **Pensione Seguso** ON THE ZATTERE   Many of the guests have stayed here many times before, and it's easy to see the appeal of the homey, old-fashioned ambience, stunning views of the Giudecca canal, and waterside terrace. *Tip:* Try to opt out of the half-board plan—you'll eat a lot better elsewhere in the neighborhood. *Fondamenta Zattere ai Geuati, Dorsoduro.* ☎ *041-5222340. 34 units. Doubles 110€–168€. AE, MC, V. Vaporetto: Zattere or Accademia. Map p 129.*

★★★ **Westin Europa and Regina** SAN MARCO   Another one of Venice's grand hotels has emerged from a cellar-to-roof renovation and adds a great deal of panache to its lovely setting on the banks of the Grand Canal near Piazza San Marco. Many of the rooms are lavishly done in a fashion that evokes the height of swanky early-20th-century decor, and the acres of silk and period pieces almost make you want to swathe yourself in evening wear and go swanning about. The terrace bar is a great place to sip a Bellini and watch the traffic on the Grand Canal. *Via XXII Marzo, San Marco.* ☎ *041-2400001. www.starwood.com. 185 units. Doubles 250€–650€. AE, DC, MC, V. Vaporetto: San Marco/Vallaresso. Map p 127.* ●

Padua (Padova)

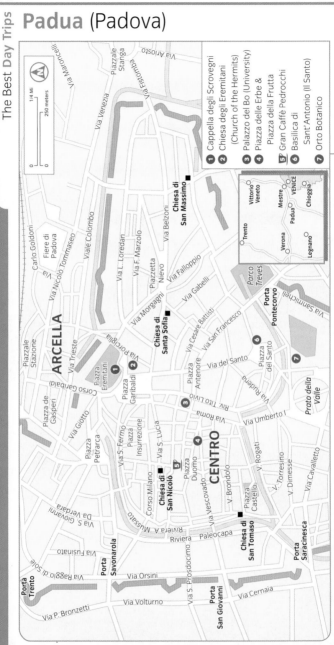

1 Cappella degli Scrovegni
2 Chiesa degli Eremitani (Church of the Hermits)
3 Palazzo del Bo (University)
4 Piazza delle Erbe & Piazza della Frutta
5 Gran Caffè Pedrocchi
6 Basilica di Sant'Antonio (Il Santo)
7 Orto Botanico

Proud Padua seems content to take a backseat to Venice, though it has plenty of treasures of its own. These include one of Europe's oldest universities, a stunning fresco cycle by Giotto, and a medieval botanical garden. **Getting there:** Padua is only 30 minutes from Venice by train, with departures about every 15 minutes. By car, take the A4 Autostrada. The tourist information office in the train station dispenses maps and other information. START: **From the train station, follow Corso di Popolo and Corso Garibaldi toward Piazza delle Erbe and the city center; the route will take you to all the major sights. You can easily tour the city on foot, and buses from the station go to the sights as well.**

❶ ★★★ Cappella degli Scrovegni.

One of the world's great painting cycles, by Giotto (1267–1337), covers the walls of what was once the chapel of the palace of the Scrovegni family. The magnificent frescoes are, in effect, atonement for the ill-gotten gains the family acquired through usury. The frescoes have been restored and are painstakingly maintained—visitors are even required to enter through a decontamination chamber. Giotto painted the frescoes from 1303–05, and in these scenes of the life of the Virgin Mary and Christ he introduced the concept of naturalism to Western painting. Biblical scenes such as Judas's betrayal of Christ with a kiss and the flight into Egypt are depicted with humanity and emotion that bring the paintings to life. *Visits restricted to 15 min. Piazza Eremitani 8, off Corso*

Giotto fresco in the Cappella degli Scrovegni.

Spectacular frescoes line the interior of the Cappella degli Scrovegni.

Garibaldi. ☎ *049-2010020. www. cappelladegliscrovegni.it. 11€ plus 1€ booking fee. Tickets must be booked in advance by going online, calling the number above, or purchase at the Padua tourist offices. Open daily 9am–10pm. Bus 3, 8, 10, 12 from train station.*

❷ ★★ Chiesa degli Eremitani (Church of the Hermits).

What's most moving about this beautifully restored 13th-century Romanesque church is what's missing—the bulk of a fresco cycle, *Life and Martyrdom of St. James and St. Christopher,* painted by Padua-born Andrea Mantegna from 1454–57. The church was leveled in a German air raid in 1944; fortunately, two of the panels had been removed for safekeeping and two others were salvaged from the rubble. 🕐 *15 min. Piazza*

The 16th-century anatomical theater in the Palazzo del Bo.

Eremitani. ☎ 049-8756410. Open daily 8:30am–12:30pm, 4:30–7pm. Bus 3, 8, 10, 12 from train station.

❸ ★★ Palazzo del Bo (University). Italy's second-oldest university, founded in 1222, has drawn such scholars as Dante, Copernicus, and Oliver Goldsmith, and was Europe's first institution of higher learning to graduate a female, Elena Lucrezia Corner Piscopia (in 1678). Guided tours of the palazzo, named for a medieval inn frequented by students and now the center of the university, show off such features as the anatomical theater from 1594

The lively markets of the Piazza delle Erbe and Piazza della Frutta.

and the battered lectern from which Galileo Galilei lectured from 1592–1610. ⏱ 1 hr. Via VIII Febbraio. ☎ 049-8275111. 3€. Open Mar–Oct Mon, Wed, Fri 3pm, 4pm, 5pm, Tues, Thurs, Sat 9am, 10am, 11am; Nov–Feb Mon, Wed, Fri 3pm, 4pm, Tues, Thurs, Sat 10am, 11am. Bus 3, 8, 12 from train station.

❹ ★★ Piazza delle Erbe & Piazza della Frutta. These two adjoining squares in the city center house one of Italy's largest and liveliest markets; produce is on offer in Piazza delle Erbe, and clothing and housewares in Piazza della Frutta. The building with the loggia rising above market stalls is the Palazzo della Ragione, built in the 13th century, rebuilt in the 15th century, and once housing the law courts. ⏱ 30 min. Piazza delle Erbe and Piazza della Frutta. Market Mon–Sat 8am–1:30pm. Bus 3, 5, 8, 9, 10, 11, 12 from train station.

❺ Gran Caffè Pedrocchi. One of Europe's legendary grand cafes, recently restored to its 19th-century grandeur, is almost a mandatory stop for a cup of coffee and panino or pastry. For an extra 3€, you can step upstairs to tour the bizarre theme rooms—but spend the euros

on another cappuccino instead.
Piazzetta Pedrocchi. ☎ *049-8781231.
Open Sun–Tues 9am–9pm; Wed–Sat
9am–midnight. Bus 3, 8, 12, 16, 18,
22 from train station.*

**❻ ★★ Basilica di Sant'Antonio
(Il Santo)** Padua is a famous pilgrimage city, and the faithful flock to this
13th-century church to honor
Anthony, a Portuguese Franciscan
friar who came to Padua around 1230
to preach against usury. Ironically, the
city's other great shrine, the Cappella
Scrovegni (see p 147), was funded
by the gains of moneylending.
Anthony's body rests in the Capella
d'Arca, surrounded by nine marble
bas-reliefs depicting scenes from his
life by Renaissance artists. The saint's
tongue is housed separately, in the
reliquary, and has been all the more
appreciated since its recent theft and
recovery. ⏱ *45 min. Piazza del Santo.*
☎ *049-8789722. www.basilica
delsanto.org. Open late Oct to Apr
daily 9am–1pm, 2–6pm; May to late
Oct daily 8:30am–1pm, 2–6:30pm.
Bus 3, 8, 12, 18 from train station.*

*The doors of the 13th century Basilica
di Sant'Antonio.*

❼ ★★ Orto Botanico. The oldest botanical garden in Europe was
founded in 1540 to provide medici-
nal herbs and plants to the university. At the center of the garden, the
oldest section, the original design
remains—beds are planted in a
circle, representing the earth,
surrounded by water. Some of the
oldest specimens include a palm
planted in 1585. ⏱ *30 min. Via Orto
Botanico 15.* ☎ *049-656614. Open
Apr–Oct daily 9am–1pm, 3–6pm.
Bus 3, 8, 12, 18 from train station.*

The Basilica di Sant'Antonio.

Verona

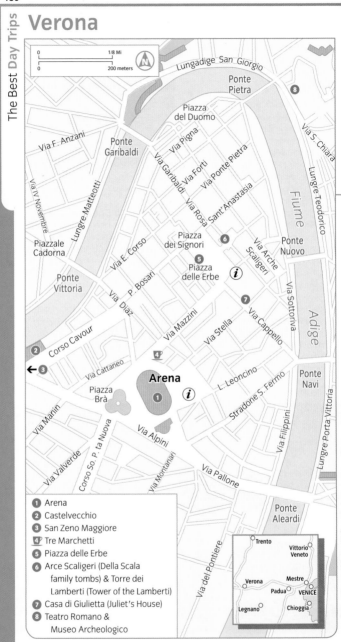

0   1/8 Mi

0   200 meters

Lungadige San Giorgio

Ponte Pietra

Piazza del Duomo

Via F. Anzani

Ponte Garibaldi

Via Pigna

Via S. Chiara

Via IV Novembre

Lungre Matteotti

Via Garibaldi

Via Forti

Via Ponte Pietra

Lungre Teodorico

Fiume

Piazzale Cadorna

Via E. Corso

Sant'Anastasia

Piazza dei Signori

Via Arche Scaligeri

Ponte Nuovo

Ponte Vittoria

P. Bosari

Via Diaz

Piazza delle Erbe

Via Rosa

Via Sottoriva

Adige

Corso Cavour

Via Mazzini

Via Stella

Via Cappello

Via Cattaneo

Arena

L. Leoncino

Ponte Navi

Piazza Brà

Stradone S. Fermo

Ponte Aleardi

Via Manin

Via Alpini

Via Filippini

Via Valverde

Corso So. P. ta Nuova

Via Montanari

Via Pallone

Lungre Porta Vittoria

Via del Pontiere

1. Arena
2. Castelvecchio
3. San Zeno Maggiore
4. Tre Marchetti
5. Piazza delle Erbe
6. Arce Scaligeri (Della Scala family tombs) & Torre dei Lamberti (Tower of the Lamberti)
7. Casa di Giulietta (Juliet's House)
8. Teatro Romano & Museo Archeologico

Trento

Vittorio Veneto

Verona

Mestre

Padua

VENICE

Legnano

Chioggia

This handsome city on the River Adige was founded by the Romans in the 1st century A.D., flourished in the Middle Ages, and was a part of the Venetian empire. Traces of this long history are much in evidence in the Roman arena, fine churches, and piazzas and palazzi, and no small part of the city's allure is the star-crossed romance of its two most famous citizens, Romeo and Juliet. **Getting there:** Verona is about 1½ to 2 hours from Venice by train, with departures about every hour. By car, take the A4 Autostrada. The tourist information office near the arena in Piazza Brà dispenses maps and other information. START: **From Verona's train station, it is about a 10-min. walk down Corso Porta Nuova to Piazza Bra and the arena, and from there Via Mazzini leads the short distance to Piazza delle Erbe and the other sites of the old city.**

① ★★ **Arena.** The best-preserved Roman arena in the world still commands the center of town. When the arena was built in the 1st century A.D., the entire population of Verona could squeeze in for gladiator shows and mock naval battles. The amphitheater is still filled to its 20,000-person capacity when operas are performed on summer evenings—a must-do experience for anyone visiting Verona at this time. ⏱ *30 min. Piazza Brà.* ☎ *045-8003204. Open Mon 1:30–7pm, Tues–Sun 8:30am–7:30pm. 3.10€.* ☎ *045-8077500 for information on opera performances. www.arena.it.*

Tickets 20€–150€. Bus 11, 12, 13 from train station.

② ★★ **Castelvecchio.** The castle of the Della Scala family, medieval rulers of Verona, looms over the River Adige. The interior was rebuilt in the 1960s by Venetian architect Carlo Scarpa, and stunning galleries house a collection of paintings by Tintoretto, Tieopolo, Guardi, and other artists whose works are usually associated with Venice. ⏱ *1 hr. Corso Castelvecchio 2.* ☎ *045-594734. 3.10€. Open Mon 1:45–7:30pm, Tues–Sun 8:30am–7:30pm. Bus 11, 12, 13 from train station.*

Cafe tables overlooking Verona's ancient Arena.

③ ★★★ San Zeno Maggiore.
One of Italy's finest Romanesque churches was built in the 12th century as a shrine to San Zeno, the first bishop of Verona and the city's beloved patron saint. Zeno's remains are enshrined behind a magnificent facade on which 12th-century sculptors Nicolò and Guglielmo portray scenes from the Bible, a theme that is carried over to the church's bronze doors. Inside, a triptych of the *Madonna and Child* by Andrea Mantegna graces the altar, and Zeno comes to life in a marble likeness that breaks the mold of religious statuary to show the famously good-natured saint chuckling. ⏱ *45 min. Piazza San Zeno.* ☎ *045-592813. 3€. Open Mar–Oct Mon–Sat 8:30am–6pm, Sun 1–6pm; Nov–Feb Tues–Sat 10am–4pm, Sun 1:30–5pm. Bus 31, 32 from train station.*

🍴 Tre Marchetti. Before heading to other sights, linger over pasta or *baccala* (salt cod, a house specialty) in atmospheric surroundings that are truly old—meals have been served here since 1291. *Vicolo Tre Marchetti.* ☎ *045-8030463.*

The church of San Zeno Maggiore.

The much-photographed balcony at Casa di Giulietta (Juliet's House).

⑤ ★ Piazza delle Erbe. The site of the Roman Forum is now Verona's central square, surrounded by palazzi and the venue for a daily market. Many of the wares on offer are of the ho-hum T-shirt variety, but enough fresh produce from the Veneto is on sale to lend an air of authenticity to the marketplace. ⏱ *30 min. Market: Mon–Sun 8:30am–7:30pm. Bus 11, 12, 13 from train station.*

⑥ ★★ Arce Scaligeri (Della Scala family tombs) & Torre dei Lamberti (Tower of the Lamberti). The tombs of the family that ruled Verona for most of the 13th and 14th centuries are masterpieces of medieval stone work. What also becomes apparent is the family's taste for bestowing canine names on other members of the family, from Mastino I (Big Mastiff, founder of the dynasty) to Cansignorio (Lord Dog, one of the last of the clan). Cangrande (Big Dog) was a patron and protector of Dante. You can see the tombs at any time through the fence without paying admission, but if you do pay for a close-up look, the same ticket allows you to ascend the nearby Torre dei Lamberti, a medieval hulk that rises 275 feet and affords stunning views. ⏱ *30 min. Via Santa Maria in Chiavica. 2.60€ for tombs and tower (elevator); 2.10€ for tombs and tower (stairs). Courtyard for close-up viewing open June–Aug Mon 1:30–7:30pm and Tues–Sun 8:30am–7:30pm. Torre dei Lamberti open Mon 1:30–7:30pm and Tues–Sun 9:30am–7:30pm Bus 11, 12, 13 from train station.*

⑦ ★ **Casa di Giulietta (Juliet's House).** Verona's shrine to love is a lovely medieval house . . . and there any authentic association with Shakespeare's heroine ends. Most shameless is the balcony from which the doomed maiden allegedly hailed Romeo, but don't be swayed—it's a 1920s addition built to capitalize on romantic appeal. ⏱ *15 min. Via Cappello 23. ☎ 045-8034303. 3.10€.*

Open Mon 1:30–7:30pm; Tues–Sun 8:30am–7:30pm. Bus 11, 12, 13 from train station.

⑧ ★★ **Teatro Romano & Museo Archeologico.** Verona's Roman theater dates from the 1st century B.C., when the outpost was an important crossroads between Rome and the northern colonies. The stone seats are built into the side of a hill, and the old city across the River Adige provides a stunning backdrop for Verona's summer festival of drama, music, and dance. An elevator ascends from the theater grounds to the cliff-top monastery that now houses the archaeological museum's small collection of statuary and other artifacts; the real draw, though, is the view over the city. ⏱ *45 min. Rigaste Redentore 2. ☎ 045-8000360. 3€. Theater open Tues–Sun 9am–7pm; museum open Mon 1:30–7pm and Tues–Sun 9am–7pm. For information on the festival, call ☎ 045-8066485 (www.estateteatraleveronese.it). Bus 31, 32, 33, 73 from train station.*

Verona's Roman theater.

Brenta Canal

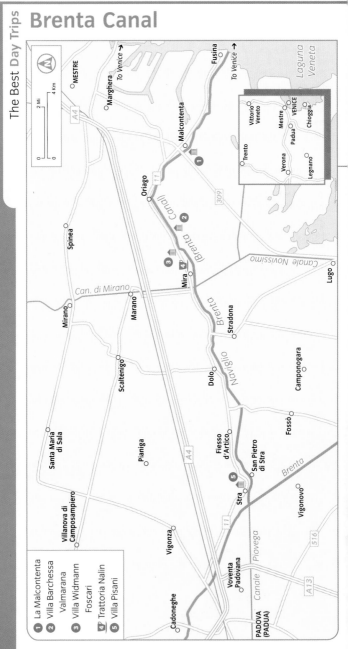

1 La Malcontenta
2 Villa Barchessa
   Valmarana
3 Villa Widmann
   Foscari
4 Trattoria Nalin
5 Villa Pisani

In the 17th and 18th centuries, Venetians of wealth and standing built summer villas along the banks of the Brenta Canal, on the mainland just west of the lagoon. Several dozen of these magnificent structures still stand on the green banks of the placid canal, and some are open to the public. Visiting them is like stepping into the grandeur of the last days of the Venetian Republic. *Tip:* Bus schedules make it difficult to see more than a few villas on a day trip—settle for a jaunt to La Malcontenta, or, if you're really ambitious, continue on from there to the village of Mira and its two nearby villas, Villa Barchessa Valmarana and Villa Widmann Foscari. START: **Begin at La Malcontenta; following Rte. S 11 by car or by bus from Venice's Piazzale Roma.**

① ★★★ **La Malcontenta.** Modeled after an ancient temple, with a classical portico that rises above the flat, grassy lowlands on a bend of the canal, Malcontenta is the most famous villa on the Brenta and one of the best-known works of the architect Andrea Palladio (see also p 46, bullets ① and ②, for other examples of this master's work). Inside are frescoes by Giambattista Zelotti and Battista Franco. The house is also known as Villa Foscari, for the family of doges who commissioned a country retreat in the 16th century; their descendants still come here in summers. According to romantic lore, the more poetic name derives from a malcontent Foscari wife exiled to the villa for an adulterous affair; more prosaically, the entire neighborhood came to be known as Malcontenta during the controversial

excavation of a canal, the *fossa dei malcontenti,* in the 15th century. 🕐 *1 hr. Via dei Turisti, Malcontenta.* ☎ *041-5470012. 8€. Open May–Oct Tues, Sat 9am–noon; open other times for groups. 53 ATVO bus or ACTV bus from Piazzale Roma to Padua.*

② ★★ **Villa Barchessa Valmarana.** The Valmaranas tore down their villa in the 19th century to avoid paying taxes, but the remaining *barchessa,* an outbuilding converted to a residence, is quite grand. The house sits amid beautiful, formal gardens on the banks of the canal and houses fine furnishings and frescoes by a student of Tiepolo. 🕐 *1 hr.* ☎ *041-424754. www.villavalmarana.net. 6€. Open Mar–Oct daily 9:30am–noon, 2:30–6pm. 53 ATVO bus or ACTV bus from Piazzale Roma to Padua.*

La Malcontenta villa.

Cruising the Brenta

The easiest way to see the Brenta is on a cruise. *Il Burchiello*, operated by the regional tourism office of Padua, stops at Villa Pisani, Barchessa Valmarana, or Villa Widmann, and Malcontenta, and pulls in for a lunch stop (meal is extra) at the village of Mira. Price includes transportation by bus back to Venice to Padua. *Via Orlandini 3, Padua.* ☎ *049-8206910. www.ilburchiello.it. 62€. Depart Venice, Pieta dock on Riva degli Schiavoni, Tues, Thurs, Sat at 9am, arrive in Padua at 6:40pm; depart Padua Wed, Fri, Sun at 8:15am, arrive in Venice at 6:20pm.*

❸ ★★ Villa Widmann Foscari. Carlo Goldoni, Igor Stravinsky, and Gabriele D'Annunzio are among the illustrious visitors to this rococo villa. They may well have enjoyed the two-story ballroom, with a minstrel's gallery and frescoes glorifying the Widman clan. ⏱ *1 hr.* ☎ *041-5600690. 5€. Open Apr Tues–Sat 10am–5pm; May–Sept daily 10am–6pm; Oct Tues–Sat 10am–5pm; Nov–Mar Sat–Sun 10am–5pm. 53 ATVO bus or ACTV bus from Piazzale Roma to Padua.*

❹ Trattoria Nalin. Enjoying a dish of risotto with scampi and a glass of crisp white from the Veneto vineyards on the flowery terrace is a perfect way to take a pause from villa viewing. *Via Nuovissimo 29, Mira.* ☎ *041-420083.*

❺ ★★ Villa Pisani. The doge Alvise Pisani built this grandiose villa to impress, a function it still fulfills. By far the grandest house on the Brenta, the villa has 114 rooms (Pisani was the 114th doge), extensive grounds, and a grand ballroom frescoed by Tiepolo; not too surprisingly, the master glorifies the Pisani family. Napoleon, who could not have been unaware of the Villa Pisani's resemblance to a French château, bought the house from the Pisani clan in 1807. Hitler and Mussolini found the villa to be a suitable venue for their first meeting, in 1939. ⏱ *1 hr.* ☎ *049-502074. 5€. Open Apr–Sept Tues–Sat 9am–7pm; Oct–Mar Tues–Sat 9am–4pm. 53 ATVO bus or ACTV bus from Piazzale Roma to Padua.* ●

The Villa Widmann Foscari.

The
Savvy Traveler

Before You Go

Italian Government Tourist Board offices

IN THE U.S.: NEW YORK: 630 Fifth Ave., Suite 1565, New York, NY 10111, ☎ 212/245-4822, fax 212/586-9249. **CHICAGO:** 500 N. Michigan Ave., Suite 2240, Chicago, IL 60611, ☎ 312/644-0996, fax 312/644-3019. **LOS ANGELES:** 12400 Wilshire Blvd., Suite 550, Los Angeles, CA 90025, ☎ 310/820-1898, fax 310/820-6367. **IN CANADA:** 175 Bloor St. E., Suite 907, South Tower, Toronto, Ontario M4W 3R8, Canada, ☎ 416/925 4882, fax 416/925 4799. **IN THE U.K.:** 1 Princes St., London W1B 2AY, ☎ (020) 7408 1254 or (09065) 508 925 (calls are charged at [£]1 per minute), fax (020) 7399 3567. **IN AUSTRALIA:** Level 4, 46 Market St. NSW 2000, Sydney, P.O. Box Q802-QVB NSW 1230, ☎ 0612/92621666, fax 0612/92621677. www.italiantourism.com.

The Best Times to Go

Try to avoid the **SUMMER MONTHS,** when the city is swamped with tourists, and the heat and humidity can be oppressive. Better times are **APRIL AND MAY** or **SEPTEMBER AND OCTOBER,** when the weather is pleasant and the crowds thinner. You may or may not want to be in Venice during **CARNEVALE,** depending on your taste for crowds and drunken revelry.

Festivals & Special Events

FEB. **Carnevale** (www.carnivalof venice.com), Venice's most famous festival, brings revelry to Venice for the 10 days before Ash Wednesday, when Lent begins. Festivities include masked processions, contests for best costumes, and fireworks. MAY. **Festa e Regata della Sensa,** a ceremony at San Nicolo on the Lido in which the mayor throws a laurel wreath into the sea, renews the Marriage of Venice to the Sea; a regatta follows. For the **Vogalonga** (www.vogalonga.com), the first Sunday after the feast of the Ascension, Venetians take to sea in all kinds of craft and row to Burano and back; anyone can participate. JUNE–NOV. **Biennale D'Arte Contemporanea e Architeturra** features art in odd years (mid-June to Nov) and architecture in even years (Sept–Oct). JULY. **Feast of Il Redentore,** third weekend of the month, commemorates the end of the plague outbreak of 1576. SEPT. For the **Regatta Storica,** first Sunday of the month, festooned boats with crews in period costumes make their way down the Grand Canal. **Mostra Internazionale d'Arte Cinematografica (the Venice International Film Festival)** is one of the world's most important and longest-running showcases for international films. NOV. **Opera season** begins at the recently rebuilt La Fenice. During the **Feast of the Madonna of the Salute,** on the 21st, religious processions cross a pontoon bridge over the Grand Canal to the church of Santa Maria della Salute.

The Weather

May, June, September, and early October are the most pleasant months. July and August can be hot and humid, and the late fall and winter can be rainy (Nov and Mar are especially bad). Damp chill can make winter months seems especially cold. High-water *(acqua alta)* tides briefly flood low-lying areas in the fall and winter months; the Piazza San Marco is one of the first areas to be submerged. When the flooding

VENICE'S AVERAGE DAILY TEMPERATURE & MONTHLY RAINFALL IN INCHES					
	JAN	FEB	MAR	APR	MAY	JUNE
Temp(°F)	43	48	53	60	67	72
Temp(°C)	6	9	12	16	19	22
Avg. Rainfall (in.)	2.3	1.5	2.9	3.0	2.8	2.9
	JULY	AUG	SEPT	OCT	NOV	DEC
Temp(°F)	77	74	68	60	54	44
Temp(°C)	25	23	29	16	12	7
Avg. Rainfall (in.)	1.5	1.9	2.9	2.6	3.0	2.1

comes, the city constructs raised walkways along major routes. (**NOTE:** Venetians wait patiently for their turn to pass along on the walkways, and it's considered extremely rude to push ahead.) Many natives wear high rubber boots when the waters hit; if you find the weather is curtailing your explorations, invest in a pair. Count on having soggy feet for just a short while: The waters usually recede in 2 or 3 hours.

Useful Websites

Venice's official tourist board site is **WWW.TURISMOVENEZIA.IT**; the city government site is **WWW.COMUNE. VENEZIA.IT**. Other useful addresses are **WWW.ITALIANTOURISM.COM** and **WWW.VENICEWORLD.COM**, a handy compilation of Venice-related sites.

How to Get the Best Airfare

Online services such as www. travelocity.com, www.expedia.com, www.orbitz.com, and www.cheap tickets.com make it easy to search for low airfares. The site www. hotwire.com provides especially low fares but with the proviso that you don't know the time of departure or routing until you book and pay. On www.priceline.com, you can name your own price for a ticket, but if your bid is accepted, you are committed to the purchase. In the U.K., www.opodo.com, www.lastminute. com, and www.discount-tickets.com offer some of the best prices on

flights. Increasingly, airlines also offer discounted fares on their websites; when traveling to Venice, for example, check out fares at www. alitalia.com, www.britishairways. com, and www.delta.com. Sunday travel sections in most newspapers also have special deals on travel, often from large travel agencies and consolidators, and some flights may be surprisingly inexpensive. Wherever you find a fare, you will get the best deal if you are flexible about the date and time of day you want to fly.

How to Get the Best Hotel Deals

You may save significantly if you book your airfare and hotel at the same time. Many of the websites mentioned above under "How to Get the Best Airfare" also offer reasonably priced hotel rooms, as does www.hotels.com. Keep in mind that most of these services require you to pay in full up front, so you may be stuck with a room you don't like (and if you don't like it when you arrive, always ask to change rooms!). Also, check with hotels to see what sort of special offers might be available directly from them (these usually appear on the hotel's website). If you see an offer on another website, call or write the hotel, mention the offer you've seen, and ask if the hotel will match it or do better—this way you will be dealing with the hotel, can request the sort of room you want, and won't be locked into a prepaid arrangement.

Cellphones (Mobiles)

Cellphones can save quite a bit of money, since they allow you to avoid high hotel phone charges. To use your cellphone in Italy, you must have a **GSM (GLOBAL SYSTEM FOR MOBILES)** cellphone with a 900 GSM frequency; this allows you to make calls anywhere in the world, though it can be expensive. It may be less expensive to rent a cellphone from an Italian provider at the airport or to purchase a prepaid phone chip to use in your phone. To rent a phone outfitted for use in Italy in advance of your trip, check www.roadpost.com or www.intouchglobal.com.

Getting **There**

By Plane

FROM NORTH AMERICA. Alitalia and Delta fly nonstop to Venice from New York's John F. Kennedy airport. Other flights from North America usually go through Milan or Rome, where they connect with flights to Venice. Travel time is about 9 hours, longer, of course, when it's necessary to make a connection. **FROM THE U.K.** British Airways flies nonstop to Venice from London and Manchester. Flying time is about 2½ hours.

Getting from the Airport to Venice

Venice's **MARCO POLO AIRPORT** is 10km (6½ miles) north of the city on the mainland.
BY BUS. The **ATVO AIRPORT SHUTTLE BUS** (☎ 041-5415180 or 041-5205530; www.atvo.it) connects with Piazzale Roma, not far from Venice's Santa Lucia train station. Buses leave from the airport about every hour and the trip costs 3€ and takes 20 minutes. The twice-hourly local public ACTV bus no. 5 (☎ 041-5415180) costs 1.50€ and takes 30 to 45 minutes. Buy tickets for either at the newsstand just inside the terminal. You can get to other parts of Venice by vaporetto from the Piazzale Roma stop.

BY TAXI. Taxis are available in front of the terminal building and the trip to Piazzale Roma costs about 30€.
BY BOAT. The **COOPERATIVE SAN MARCO/ALILAGUNA** (☎ 041-5235775; www.alilaguna.it) operates a large *motoscafo* (shuttle boat) service from the airport with two stops at Murano and the Lido before arriving after about 1 hour in Piazza San Marco; the trip costs 10€. The fee for a private water taxi is a legal minimum of 55€, but the fare is usually closer to 75€ for two to four passengers with few bags; water taxis are usually available at the landing outside the airport or contact the **CORSORZIO MOTOSCAFI VENEZIA** (☎ 041-5222303; www. motoscafivenezia.it).

By Car

Large car parks at the entrance to the city include the **GARAGE SAN MARCO,** Piazzale Roma (☎ 041-5232213), about 26€ for 24 hours and **ISOLA DEL TRONCHETTO** (☎ 041-5207555), about 18€ a day. It is less expensive to park on the mainland at Mestre, where options include **PARKING STAZIONE** (☎ 041-938021), about 4.50€ a day, and take the train from there.

By Train
STAZIONE VENEZIA-SANTA LUCIA, Venice's train station, is 5½ hours from Rome, 4 hours from Florence, 3½ hours from Milan, and 2 hours from Bologna. The Ferrovia vaporetto stop is on the Grand Canal in front of the station.

By Bus
Buses arrive at the Piazzale Roma. For schedules, call ☎ 041-5287886.

Getting **Around**

By Vaporetto
Vaporetti (water buses) connect points along the Grand Canal, other areas of the city, and islands. Boats run every 10 or 15 minutes from 7am to midnight, and once an hour after midnight until morning. An *accelerato* makes every stop; a *diretto* makes express stops. A one-way ticket is 3.50€, a round-trip ticket is 6€, and a 24-hour ticket is 11€. Tickets are also available for all travel within 3 days (22€) and a week (32€). Tickets are available at stops, from newsstands and tobacco shops, and from ACTV and VeLa offices (see below). You must stamp your ticket in one of the machines at each stop; you can also pay on board, for a 1€ supplement. Do pay, though—if you're caught without a ticket the fine is a steep 21€. For information, contact **ACTV (AZIENDA DEL CONSORZIO TRASPORTI VENEZIANO),** Calle Fuseri 1810, off the Frezzeria in San Marco (☎ 041-5287886, www.actv.it; Mon–Sat 7:30am–7pm), or **VELA,** Piazzale Roma (☎ 041-2722249; www.velaspa.com; daily 7:30am–8pm).

By Traghetti
Traghetti are large, unadorned gondolas rowed by standing gondoliers across the Grand Canal. The ride is reasonably priced at .50€, but if you do as the Venetians do and stand as you are ferried across the water, it can be a bit of a challenge. Some popular traghetti crossings are between Fondamente del Vin to Riva del Carbòn (Mon–Sat 8am–2pm) and the Pescaria and Santa Sofia (Mon–Sat 7:30am–8:30pm; Sun 8am–7pm), both near the Rialto. An especially scenic ride is that between San Marco and the Dogana (daily 9am–noon, 2–6pm).

By Water Taxi
Taxi acquei (water taxis) are expensive: 14€ for trips up to 7 minutes and .25€ for each 15 seconds thereafter. Each bag over 50 centimeters long costs 1.15€, plus there's a 4.40€ supplement for service from 10pm–7am and a 4.65€ surcharge for travel on Sunday and holidays. These rates are for four people; add 1.60€ for each extra passenger. You'll find water-taxi stations at: the Ferrovia, ☎ 041-716286; Piazzale Roma, ☎ 041-716922; the Rialto Bridge, ☎ 041-5230575 or 041-723112; Piazza San Marco, ☎ 041-5229750; the Lido, ☎ 041-5260059; and Marco Polo Airport, ☎ 041-5415084. Call **RADIO TAXI** (☎ 041-5222303 or 041-723112) for a pickup anywhere in the city; a surcharge of 4.15€ is added.

By Gondola
If your fantasies involve hearing "O Solo Mio" as you float down the Grand Canal, expect to pay 62€ for up to 50 minutes (77€ between 8pm and 8am), with up to six passengers, and 31€ for each additional 25 minutes (39€ between

8pm and 8am). There are 12 gondola stations around the city, including those at Piazzale Roma, the train station, the Rialto Bridge, and Piazza San Marco. Gondolas are regulated by the **ENTE GONDOLA** (☎ 041-5285075; www.gondolavenezia.it).

On Foot
Walking is the only way to explore Venice, and a delightful experience. Throngs of tourists crowd San Marco, but you may get the impression that few venture beyond it. Yellow signs direct you to the major city points. Carry a detailed map of the city (*pianta della città*), which can be purchased at newsstands and bookstores. No matter how carefully you follow a map, time after time you'll find yourself lost—enjoy the experience of simply wandering. Venetians are extremely polite when asked for directions, so if you become worrisomely lost, ask for help: *Mi scusi, siamo perduti. Desideriamo andare a . . .* (Excuse me, we're lost. We want to go to . . .).

Fast **Facts**

AMERICAN EXPRESS   The main office is on Salizzada San Moisè, just west of Piazza San Marco, ☎ 041-5200844. Summer, banking: Mon–Sat, 8am–8pm, other services: 9am–5:30pm; winter, all services, Mon–Fri, 9am–5:30pm, Sat, 9am–noon.

APARTMENT RENTALS   Resources for apartment rentals of a week or more are www.veniceapartment.com, www.vaporettovenice.com, and www.interflats.it.

ATMS   ATMs (automated teller machines) are located throughout the city. Italy uses 4-digit PINs; if you have a 6-digit number, change it at your bank before you leave.

BABYSITTING   Ask your hotel to help you arrange a babysitter.

BANKING HOURS   Banks are open Monday to Friday, 8:20am to 1:20pm and 2:45 to 3:45pm and closed on holidays.

BIKE RENTALS   Venice is not for cyclists—in fact, biking is forbidden to adults in the city. However, bikes are available on the Lido through Bruno Lazzari, Gran Viale 21B, Lido, (☎ 041-5268019). March to September daily 8am–8pm; October to February daily 8:30am to 1pm and 3 to 7:30pm.

BUSINESS HOURS   Shops are open Monday to Saturday, 9am to 12:30pm and 3 to 7:30pm. Most businesses are closed on Sunday; in winter they close on Monday morning, and in summer usually on Saturday afternoon. Grocers are usually closed on Wednesday afternoon. Many restaurants close on holidays, sometime in July or August for a holiday, frequently over Christmas, and often for a week or so in January before Carnevale.

CONSULATES   **U.S.:** In Milan, Largo Donegani 1, ☎ 02-290351, Monday to Friday, 9am to noon for visas; Monday to Friday, 2 to 4pm for telephone info. **U.K:** In Venice, Campo della Carità, Dorsoduro 1051, ☎ 041-522-7207 (near the Accademia bridge, in the Palazzo Querini); Monday to Friday 9am to noon and 2 to 4pm.

CREDIT CARDS   Visa and MasterCard are widely accepted; many businesses also accept American Express. You may be able to have a PIN assigned by your bank so that you can use your card at ATMs.

CUSTOMS   Citizens of non-EU countries are allowed to bring the following into Italy duty-free: 200 cigarettes or 50 cigars or 250 grams of tobacco; 1 liter of spirits or 2 liters of wine; 50 grams of perfume. On leaving Italy, U.S. citizens who have been abroad for at least 48 hours are entitled to bring home $400 worth of duty-free merchandise. Be sure to keep receipts of all your purchases. Citizens of other EU countries do not need to declare goods.

DENTISTS & DOCTORS   Check with the consulate of the United States or the United Kingdom, the American Express office, or your hotel.

DRESS   Legs and shoulders should be covered when entering churches. Women may want to carry a scarf to cover their heads.

DRUGSTORES   Regular hours are Monday to Friday 9am to 12:30pm and 3:45 to 7:30pm; Saturday 9am to 12:45pm. Pharmacies take turns staying open all night; a sign posted outside all pharmacies indicates which pharmacy is currently remaining open.

ELECTRICITY   Electrical current is 220V AC, with two- or three-pronged plugs. You will need a transformer for most electrical appliances you bring with you, and also an adapter for electrical outlets.

EMERGENCIES   Dial ☎ **113** to reach the police, ☎ **115** to report a fire, and ☎ **118** to summon an ambulance and/or emergency medical assistance. The agency **Venezia No Problem** can help you if you feel you've been treated unfairly or extremely rudely by a shopkeeper or hotelier. Call toll-free at ☎ 800-355920.

HOLIDAYS   Offices, shops, and many restaurants are closed on the following holidays: January 1, New Year's Day; Easter Monday; April 25, Liberation Day and the feast day of St. Mark, the city's patron; May 1, Labor Day; August 15, Assumption of the Virgin; November 1, All Saints Day; December 8, Feast of the Immaculate Conception; December 25,

Christmas; and December 26, feast day of St. Stephen.

HOSPITALS   **Ospedale Civile Santi Giovanni e Paolo,** on Campo Santi Giovanni e Paolo, has English-speaking staff and provides emergency service 24 hours a day (☎ 041-785111; vaporetto: San Tomà). For an ambulance and emergency medical aid, dial ☎ **118.**

INSURANCE   Check with you health insurance plan to see if you are covered while traveling abroad. If not, you can purchase travel insurance policies that cover health care abroad and often transportation back home if necessary.

INTERNET ACCESS   Internet cafes are quite common in Venice, and make it easy to log on to the Internet and check e-mail. Among them are **Internet Café,** Campo Santo Stefano (☎ 041-5208128; daily 24 hr.; 9€ an hour; Vaporetto: San Samuele); and **Venetian Navigator,** Calle delle Bande between San Marco and Campo Santa Maria Formosa (☎ 041-5226084; May–Oct daily 10am–10pm; Nov–Apr daily 10am–1pm, 2:30–8:30pm; 6€ an hour; Vaporetto: Rialto).

LOST AND FOUND   The central **Ufficio Oggetti Rinvenuti (Lost and Found office)** is in the annex to the City Hall (Municipio) on Calle Piscopia o Loredan, just off Riva del Carbon on the Grand Canal, near the Rialto Bridge (☎ 041-788225; Mon, Wed, Fri 9:30am–12:30pm; Vaporetto: Rialto).

MAIL   You can buy stamps *(francobolli)* at tobacconists *(tabacchi).* The central post office is on the San Marco side of the Rialto Bridge at Rialto: **Fondaco dei Tedeschi:** Monday to Saturday; stamps available 8:30am–6:30pm, other services, 8:10am–1:30pm (☎ 041-2717111 or 041-5285813; Vaporetto: Rialto). Postal services are also available near Piazza San Marco on Calle Larga dell'Ascensione (Mon–Fri 8:30am–2pm; Sat 8:30am–1pm).

MONEY   The euro is Italy's official currency. Euro banknotes come in denominations of 5€, 10€, 20€, 100€, 200€, and 500€ and coins of .2€, .5€, .10€, .20€, .50€, 1€, and 2€.

POLICE   In an emergency, dial ☎ **112** or ☎ **113**.

SAFETY   Venice is one of Italy's safest cities. Beware, however, of pickpockets in crowds in the streets or on the *vaporetti* and of occasional thievery at night in the dark, back streets. As is the case anywhere, common sense is your best protection.

SENIOR TRAVELERS   Members of **AARP (American Association of Retired Persons)** are often eligible for discounts on airfare, hotels, and car rentals. If you are 50 or older, consider becoming a member before traveling; 601 E. St., NW, Washington, DC 20049 (☎ 800/424-3410; www.aarp.org). Many seniors also enjoy tours with **Elderhostel**, 11 Avenue de Lafayette, Boston, MA 02111 (☎ 877/426-8056; www.elderhostel.org), and **Interhostel**, University of New Hampshire, 6 Garrison Ave., Durham, NH 03824 (☎ 800/733-9753; www.learn.unh.edu/interhostel). Both organizations provide escorted tours, with an emphasis on lectures and field trips, are relatively inexpensive, and provide an excellent opportunity to meet like-minded travelers.

SMOKING   Smoking is prohibited in public buildings and on public transportation, and an increasing number of restaurants and bars either prohibit smoking or provide no-smoking sections.

TAXES   Like all members of the European Union, Italy has a value-added tax (VAT), called IVA. On your hotel bills the IVA will range from 9% to 19%, depending on whether your room is first or second class or

luxury. IVA is automatically included in the cost of goods you buy. If you are from a non-European Union country and spend more than 150€ in a store, you are entitled to reimbursement of the IVA. Ask for an invoice at the store, then take it to the customs office at the airport and have it stamped while you are still in Italy. Once home, send the vendor the stamped invoice. Eventually he or she will send you your refund. Be sure to make a copy of the invoice before you mail it. If you made your purchase with a credit card you can ask that the card be credited. Many stores now belong to a "Tax Free for Tourists" plan (look for stickers in the window) and will issue a check when you pay for your purchase. At the airport, have the check validated by customs, then cash the check in the Tax Free booth. You can also mail it back within 60 days.

TELEPHONES   Most public phones in Venice require that you use a phone card *(schede telefoniche),* available at newsstands, bars, and elsewhere. To make a call, tear off one corner of the card as indicated and insert it in the appropriate slot. Even when calling within Venice, you will need to dial the prefix, 041. You can also purchase phone cards for international calls *(schede telefoniche internazionali).* When making international calls, dial 00, country code, area code (without the initial zero), then the number. Some country codes are: Australia, 61; New Zealand, 64; U.K., 44; U.S., 1. You can also make international calls using phone cards provided by AT&T and other providers. To do so, dial the card access number; country code, area code and number, and your calling card number. Avoid making calls from your hotel room, as these can be quite expensive. Access numbers for some common providers are: AT&T (☎ 172-1011),

MCI (☎ 172-1022), and Sprint (☎ 172-1877).

TIPPING   In restaurants, a 15% service charge is typically included on your bill *(servizio incluso)*, but leave a little extra (a euro or two) if the service has been good. Give checkroom attendants .75€ and washroom attendants .25€ to .35€. A service charge is also included in your hotel bill, but give the chambermaid 1€ for each day of your stay and the porter 1.50€ to 2.50€ for carrying your bags. A concierge expects tips for any extra service he or she provides.

TOILETS   Public toilets are marked by blue and green WC signs. There is a fee of about .50€. *Signori* means men; *signore*, women; when looking for a toilet, ask for *il bagno*.

TOURIST OFFICES IN VENICE   The government-run **APT** is in Piazza San Marco (☎ 041-5226356 or 041-5298730). This office and branches throughout the city supply free maps, as well as information on sights concerts, exhibitions, and other events. Tourist offices also provide hotel listings. Branches are in the train station, in Piazzale Roma, and on the Lido, at Viale Santa Maria Elisabetta (☎ 041-5265721). The main office is open daily 9:30am to 3:30pm; vaporetto: San Marco/Vallaresso.

TRAVELERS WITH DISABILITIES   Venice, city of bridges and stairs, can be difficult for almost anyone to navigate, especially those with physical disabilities. Some of the city's 400 bridges have been outfitted with mechanized lifts for wheelchairs, but most still involve a climb up and down steps at either end or navigating a steep incline. Italian law has done much to regulate wheelchair accessibility to hotels, restrooms, restaurants, and museums, but not all are wheelchair accessible; it's essential that you call ahead of time to verify accessibility. *Vaporetti* provide relatively easy access for wheelchairs. The tourist office provides a free map showing wheelchair-accessible sights, and two excellent online sources for information about accessible travel are **Moss Rehab ResourceNet** (www.mossresourcenet.org) and **Access-Able Travel Source** (www.access-able.com).

TRAVELER'S CHECKS   ATMs have made traveler's checks a bit of an anachronism, but if you want to use them, call: American Express, ☎ 800/721-9768 in the U.S. and Canada, www.americanexpress.com; Thomas Cook, ☎ 800/223-7373 in the U.S. and Canada, or ☎ 44/1733-318-950 from anywhere else (call collect), www.thomascook.com; Visa, ☎ 800/227-6811 in the U.S. and Canada, or ☎ 44/0207-937-8091 from anywhere else (call collect), www.visa.com; or Citicorp (☎ 800/645-6556 in the U.S. and Canada, or 813/623-1709 from anywhere else (call collect). To report lost or stolen traveler's checks in Italy, call toll-free: American Express, ☎ 800/872-000; Thomas Cook, ☎ 800/872-050; Visa, ☎ 800/874-155.

Venice: A Brief History

400–600 Refugees flee barbarians on the mainland to islands in the lagoon.

421 According to tradition, Venice was founded on April 25, the feast day of St. Mark, patron saint of Venice.

639 Torcello's cathedral begun.

697 According to legend, first doge elected.

729 Doge attempts to form a hereditary monarchy. Civil war ensues until the doge is murdered.

814 First Palazzo Ducale begun.

828 Body of St. Mark stolen from Alexandria.

834 First Basilica di San Marco begun.

867 Torcello's cathedral rebuilt.

1000 Venice begins to become a maritime power.

1008 Torcello's cathedral rebuilt again.

1094 Basilica di San Marco consecrated.

1095 Venice furnishes ships and supplies for the First Crusade.

1171 The six districts of Venice are established.

1173 First Rialto bridge built.

1204 The Sack of Constantinople. Venice's booty includes four bronze horses now in Basilica di San Marco.

1255 Wars with Genoa.

1309 Today's Palazzo Ducale begun.

1310 Venetian Constitution is passed; the Council of Ten instituted.

1348–49 The plague (Black Death) cuts the city's population in half.

1380 Venice wins maritime supremacy in the Mediterranean and Adriatic; conquers Cyprus.

1453 Venice's Empire reaches its peak after Constantinople falls to the Turks; Venice's power begins to wane.

1489 Venice conquers Cyprus.

1514 Fire destroys the Rialto bridge.

1516 Ghetto founded.

1630 The Black Death strikes again, reducing population to its smallest in 250 years.

1718 Venetian maritime empire ends.

1792 La Fenice opera house opens.

1797 Napoleon invades the Veneto; Venetian Republic ends.

1798 Napoleon gives Venice to Austria.

1804 Napoleon crowned king of Italy.

1848 Venice revolts against Austria.

1849 Venetian troops surrender.

1866 Venice freed from Austrian rule; united with the kingdom of Italy.

1870–1900 Industry grows. Railway bridge linking Venice to the mainland built. Tourism begins to flourish.

1895 First Biennale D'Arte.

1902 Campanile in Piazza San Marco collapses.

1966 Venice devastated by floods. Discussions on how to save the fragile city become heated.

1996 Teatro La Fenice destroyed by fire.

2002 Mobile tide barriers to control tidal damage completed.

2003 La Fenice reopens.

Venetian **Art & Architecture**

Venice has inspired artists since the city's earliest beginnings.
Their works fill churches, *scuole* (guild halls), and the city's museums,
and to spend time in front of these works is reason alone to come to
Venice.

MOSAICS   Venice's first burst of artistic expression came by way of Byzantium and Ravenna, when, in the 12th century, artisans began decorating the interiors of **BASILICA DI SAN MARCO** and the **BASILICA DI SANTA MARIA ASSUNTA** on **TORCELLO** with brilliant mosaics. Even though many of the original tiles have been replaced or badly restored over the years, enough remain to create a magical, ever-changing environment.

PAOLO VENEZIANO (active 1320–65) Venetian art made a great step forward when the *Coronation of the Virgin* (in the Accademia) and other works by this artist appeared, displaying fluid lines, lack of strict formality in the composition, and bright, opulent colors, all marking a move away from the Byzantine.

GIOVANNI BELLINI (1430–1516) Bellini brought Venetian painting to the threshold of the Renaissance, and the step forward is especially noteworthy in *Madonna with Saints* in the church of San Zaccaria. The colors are mellow and rich, and light illuminates the figures, which stand out as individuals rather than stock decoration.

GIORGIONE (1477–1510)   When you enter Room 5 in the Accademia and see the *Tempest,* one of the most mysterious paintings in Western art, you move into another world—and understand why Giorgione is considered to be the first modern artist. A storm approaches, a sensuous, lyrical mood pervades, color and light fill the painting, and landscape and drama take center stage.

TITIAN (1485?–1576)   It is said that Titian was so highly regarded that when Charles V visited his studio and the artist dropped his brush, the emperor picked it up. During his long career Titian made breakthroughs in color and light, created dazzling, luminous effects with glazes, and experimented with composition. All these elements are evident in *Madonna with Saints and Members of the Pesaro Family* in the Scuole Santa Maria Gloriosa dei Frari. Here, Titian takes a conventional subject and turns it upside down, moving the Madonna from the center of the composition to the upper right side of the painting; other figures forming a strong diagonal moving toward her, and brilliant light and color envelop the entire painting.

TINTORETTO (1518–94)   This native Venetian worked passionately, using a wide brush and priming the canvases with dark tones, then bringing out the lights. In his *Last Supper* in San Giorgio Maggiore and other works you see Tintoretto's use of light and his focus on everyday scenes.

PAOLO VERONESE (1528–88)   In the Venetian world of Veronese, robust men and women dressed in sumptuous clothing move about in marble settings, obviously enjoying life and awash in bright blues and yellows and violets and pinks. Typical is *Christ in the House of Levi* in the Accademia, in which a holy event is depicted as a secular scene—to such an extent that this painting of the Last Supper was considered to be blasphemous.

GIAMBATTISTA PIAZZETTA (1682–1754) Religious zeal hits new heights in such works as *Glorification of Saint Dominic* in the church of Santi Giovanni e Paolo, in which figures ascend into the swirling heavens.

GIAMBATTISTA TIEPOLO (1696–1770) The master of the Venetian baroque is best known for his colorful frescoes in Palazzo Labia and other Venetian churches and palaces.

CANALETTO (1697–1768), **PIETRO LONGHI** (1702–58), **FRANCESCO GUARDI** (1712–93) These three artists of the 18th century shifted the focus from religion to secular, even everyday subjects. Canaletto's views of the Grand Canal, Longhi's scenes of balls and other social gatherings, and Guardi's paintings of the Lagoon hang in the Museo del Settecento Veneziano.

Fleeing barbarian hordes on the mainland, the first settlers on the Venetian lagoon established a colony on the island of Torcello, where they soon began work on a cathedral. Venice would continue to take shape for the next thousand years, reaching new heights of architectural achievement with the passing centuries.

BYZANTINE Founded in the 7th century, rebuilt in the 9th, altered in the 11th, Torcello cathedral still stands as the best example of the city's Byzantine past. A Greek-cross plan, covered porch, marble columns, splendid mosaics, and other telltale signs of the Byzantine are much in evidence here and in the adjoining church of Santa Fosca.

GOTHIC The Palazzo Ducale, begun in the 14th century and built over several centuries, beautifully exemplifies the hallmark Gothic elements: pointed arches, skillful ornament and tracery, pierced quatrefoil decoration, and capitals atop the columns. Venice's fine Venetian-Gothic palaces

include the Ca' d'Oro, which architect Bartolomeo Bon (1374–1464) imbued with elegant tracery, opulent detail, color, and a richly decorated facade.

THE RENAISSANCE Balance and symmetry, hallmarks of Renaissance painting and architecture, are in many ways antithetical to the Venetian love of color and ornamentation. The exquisite church of Santa Maria dei Miracoli is a good example of how architect Pietro Lombardo (1435–1515) balanced the two sensibilities. Panels of richly colored marble glisten in the Venetian light and tie the church to the Gothic style, but classical rounded arches, beautifully balanced proportions, and a soaring dome are perfectly in keeping with Renaissance ideals.

The great architect Andrea Palladio (1508–80) spent several years in Rome studying its ruins, and classical elements—balance, proportion, and harmony—are much in evidence in two of Venice's finest churches, San Giorgio Maggiore and Il Redentore. More Palladian classicism graces the shores of the Brenta Canal, where the villas he built for Venetian aristocracy resemble temples. Sansovino (1486–1570) fled to Venice after the sack of Rome, bringing with him an appreciation of the classical that appears in the Marciana Library and other buildings around the Piazza San Marco.

BAROQUE Baldassare Longhena (1598–1682) is Venice's master of the baroque, and he described his greatest creation, the church of Santa Maria della Salute, as "strange, worthy, and beautiful." The church is massive, topped by domes inspired by St. Peter's in Rome. The theatrical exterior is decorated with sculpture, and the octagonal form creates an exuberant and dynamic pattern; the interior is remarkable for its huge central space.

DISCOUNT CARDS

The **VENICE CARD** can help make your trip to Venice slightly more affordable by providing discounts throughout the city. You must purchase your card at least 24 hours in advance. Call outside of Italy (☎ 39/041-2424), or go online (www.venicecard.com). The Blu ticket allows free passage on buses and vaporetti, use of public toilets, and a reduced daily rate of 6.70€, along with a reserved spot, at the public ASM parking garage, and a price of 5€ for the pass to the churches. The Orange card includes admission to many museums and lets you avoid long lines. Another version pays for passage into Venice from the airport, but it won't save you any money. For adults, the Blu card costs 14€ for 1 day, 29€ for 3 days, or 51€ for 7 days; for ages 4 to 29, the Blu card costs 9€ for 1 day, 22€ for 3 days, or 49€ for 7 days. For adults, the Orange card costs 28€ for 1 day, 47€ for 3 days, or 68€ for 7 days; for ages 4 to 29, the Orange card costs 18€ for 1 day, 35€ for 3 days, or 61€ for 7 days. Buy in advance by phone or online.

A great buy for visitors between 14 and 29 is the **ROLLING VENICE PASS.** For only 3€ (and the pass lasts until Dec 31 of the year issued) the card provides discounts at selected hotels and restaurants, and shops, plus reduced entrance fees to museums, and 3-day vaporetto passes. There's a Rolling Venice office in the train station from July through September daily 8am to 8pm; in winter you can get the pass at the Transalpino travel agency just outside the station's front doors and to the right, at the top of the steps, open Monday to Friday 8:30am to 12:30pm and 3 to 7pm and Saturday 8:30am to 12:30pm.

Useful Phrases & Menu Terms

Phrases

ENGLISH	ITALIAN	PRONUNCIATION
Thank you	Grazie	**graht**-tzee-ay
Please	per favore	pehr-fah-**vohr**-eh
Yes	sì	see
No	no	noh
Good morning	buongiorno	bwahn-**djor**-noh
Good evening	buona sera	**bwahn**-oh **serr**-ah
How are you?	Come sta?	koh-may-**stah**
I'm well	Molto bene	**mohl**-toh-**bhen**-eh
Excuse me	Scusi	**skoo**-zee
Where is?	Dovè	doh-**veh**
a hotel	un albergo	oon ahl-**behr**-goh
a restaurant	un ristorante	oon reest-ohr-**ahnt**-ey
the bathroom	il bagno	eel **bahn**-nyah
To the right	A destra	ah **dehy**-stra
To the left	A sinistra	ah see-**nees**-tra

ENGLISH	ITALIAN	PRONUNCIATION
Straight ahead	Avanti	ahv-**vahn**-tee
Good	buono	**bwoh**-noh
Bad	cattivo	ka-**tee**-voh
Open	aperto	ah-**pair**-toh
Closed	chiuso	kee-**oo**-soh
Hot	caldo	**kahl**-doh
Cold	freddo	**fray**-doh
Big	grande	**gran**-day
Expensive	caro	**kahr**-roh
Cheap	a buon prezza	ah bwon **pretz**-so
Small	piccolo	**pee**-koh-loh
I'm sorry.	Mi dispiace.	**mee**-dis-pach-e-ray
Do you speak English?	Parla inglese?	par-la in-**glay**-say
I would like?	Vorrei?	**vor**-ray
How much does it cost?	Quanto costa?	**kwanto**-kosta

Emergencies

ENGLISH	ITALIAN	PRONUNCIATION
Help!	Aiuto!	eye-**yooh**-toh
Call the police!	Chiama la polizia	kee-ah-mah lah poh-**lee**-tsee-ah
a doctor	un medico	oon **meh**-dee-koh
an ambulance	un ambulanza	oon am-boo-**lehn**-tsah

Numbers

ENGLISH	ITALIAN	PRONUNCIATION
1	uno	**oo**-noh
2	due	**doo**-ay
3	tre	**tray**
4	quattro	**kwah**-troh
5	cinque	**ceen**-kway
6	sei	say
7	sette	**set**-tay
8	otto	**oh**-toh
9	nove	**noh**-vay
10	dieci	dee-**ay**-chee
11	undici	**oon**-dee-chee
12	dodici	**do**-dee-chee
13	tredici	**tray**-dee-chee
14	quattordici	kwah-troh-**dee**-chee
15	quindici	**kwin**-dee-cee
16	sedici	**say**-dee-cee
17	diciassette	dee-cee-a-**set**-tay
18	diciotto	dee-cee-**oh**-toh
19	diciannove	dee-cee-ah-**noh**-vay
20	venti	**vehn**-tee

ENGLISH	ITALIAN	PRONUNCIATION
30	trenta	**treyn**-tah
40	quaranta	kwah-**rahn**-tah
50	cinquanta	cheen-**kwan**-tah
60	sessanta	sehs-**sahn**-tah
70	settanta	seht-**tahn**-tah
80	ottanta	oht-**tan**-tah
90	novanta	noh-**vahnt**-tah
100	cento	**chen**-toh
1000	mille	**mee**-lay
2000	duemila	doo-ay-**mee**-lay
5000	cinquemila	ceen-kway-**mee**-la

Days of the Week

ENGLISH	ITALIAN	PRONUNCIATION
Monday	Lunedi	**loo**-nay-dee
Tuesday	Martedi	**mart**-ay-dee
Wednesday	Mercoledi	**mehr**-cohl-ay-dee
Thursday	Giovedi	joh-**vay**-dee
Friday	Venerdi	ven-**nehr**-dee
Saturday	Sabato	sah-**bah**-tah
Sunday	La Domenica	lah doh-mehn-**nee**-kah

Restaurant Phrases

Have you a table for___?	Avete una tavola per____?
I would like____.	Vorrei_____.
A glass of_____	Un bicchiere di
mineral water	acqua minerale
carbonated water	gassata
uncorbonated water	senza gas
white wine	vino bianco
red wine	vino rosso
beer	birra
First course	il primo
Main course	il secondo
The bill please.	Il conto, per favore.
Is the service included?	è incluso il servizio?

Menu Items

ENGLISH	ITALIAN	PRONUNCIATION
Anchovies	Acciughe	ah-**choo**-gay
Artichokes	Carciofi	kar-**chof**-fee
Beans	Fagioli	fah-**joh**-lee
Beef	Manzo	**man**-zoh
Butter	Burro	**boor**-roh
Cheeses	Formaggi	for-**mahd**-jee
Chicken	Pollo	**po**-lo
Clams	Vongole	**vahn**-goh-lee
Consomme	Brodo	**bro**-doh
Desserts	Dolci	**dol**-chee

ENGLISH	ITALIAN	PRONUNCIATION
Eggplant	Melanzana	*meh-lan-__tsah__-nee*
Eggs	Uova	*__woh__-vah*
Fish	Pesce	*__pech__-ay*
Lamb	Agnello	*ahn-__yell__-oh*
Liver	Fegato	*fay-__gah__-toh*
Meat sauce	Ragu	*rah-__goo__*
Mushrooms	Funghi	*__foon__-gee*
Nuts	Noci	*__no__-chee*
Pork	Maiale	*may-__ah__-lay*
Rice	Riso	*__ree__-so*
Sardines	Sarde	*__sar__-day*
Sauce	Salsa	*__sahl__-sa*
Sausages	Salsiccie	*sahl-see-__chee__-ay*
Shrimp	Gamberoni	*gam-ber-__oh__-nee*
Snails	Lumache	*loo-__mah__-chay*
Soup	Zuppa	*__zoo__-pah*
Steak	Bistecca	*__bee__-stek-kah*
Tomatoes	Pomodori	*pah-mo-__dor__-ee*
Veal	Vitello	*vi-__tell__-oh*
Vegetables	Contorni	*kan-__tor__-nee*
Vinegar	Aceto	*ah-__chay__-toh*

Index

Photo **Credits**

Frommers.com

So many places, so little time?

TOKYO 7766 miles

LONDON 3818 miles

TORONTO 4682 miles

SYDNEY 5087 miles

NEW YORK 4947 miles

LOS ANGELES 2556 miles

HONG KONG 5638 miles

Frommers.com makes the going fast and easy.

Find a destination. ✓ Buy a guidebook. ✓ Book a trip. ✓ Get hot travel deals.
Enter to win vacations. ✓ Check out the latest travel news.
Share trip photos and memories. ✓ And much more.

Frommers.com
Rated #1 Travel Web Site by *PC Magazine*®